And Evermore Shall Be So

A play

Norman Robbins

Samuel French — London
www.samuelfrench-london.co.uk

CHARACTERS

Ida Cornish
Sheila Pashley
David Lilywhite
Helen Lilywhite
Roy Steadman
Lydia Summerfield
Rev. Edwin Summerfield
Brandon Walsh
Maurice Walker
Gwendoline Cranshawe

SYNOPSIS OF SCENES

ACT I
SCENE 1 A Wednesday morning in early September
SCENE 2 The following Tuesday

ACT II
SCENE 1 A few hours later. Evening
SCENE 2 Six weeks later. Wednesday morning
SCENE 3 Thursday evening

The action of the play takes place in the living room of Glebe House, a rambling Victorian vicarage, presently occupied by the Rev. Edwin Summerfield and his wife

Time: The present

Other plays and pantomimes by
Norman Robbins
published by Samuel French Ltd

At the Sign of "The Crippled Harlequin"
Aladdin
Ali Baba and the Forty Thieves
Babes in the Wood
Cinderella
Dick Whittington
The Grand Old Duke of York
Hansel and Gretel
Hickory Dickory Dock
Humpty Dumpty
Jack and Jill
Jack and the Beanstalk
The Late Mrs Early
Nightmare
Prescription for Murder
Pull the Other One
Puss in Boots
Red Riding Hood
Rumpelstiltzkin
Sing a Song of Sixpence
Slaughterhouse
Sleeping Beauty
Snow White
Tiptoe Through the Tombstones
Tom, the Piper's Son
Tomb with a View
Wedding of the Year
The White Cat
The Wonderful Story of Mother Goose

For

Vivien Goodwin

I'll sing you twelve, O
Green grow the rushes, O
What are your twelve, O?
Twelve for the twelve Apostles,
Eleven for the eleven who went to heaven,
Ten for the ten commandments,
Nine for the nine bright shiners,
Eight for the eight bold rangers,
Seven for the seven stars in the sky
Six for the six proud walkers,
Five for the symbols at your door,
Four for the Gospel makers,
Three, three, the rivals,
Two, two, lilywhite boys,
Clothèd all in green, O-O
One is one and all alone
And evermore shall be so.

Anon

ACT I

Scene 1

The living-room of Glebe House, a rambling Victorian vicarage in Athelston, near Norwich. A Wednesday morning in early September

The room, though large and airy, has a tired look to it, and is in need of redecorating. The entrance to the room is through the heavy-looking door far L of the rear wall. When this is opened, a glimpse of the dingy hall can be seen. This runs behind the rear wall, leading R to the kitchen and the back of the house, and L, to the staircase, dining-room and study. The wall R, is dominated by huge french windows. These are framed by heavy drapes with matching pelmet. A mature garden may be glimpsed. Below the french windows is a record and CD cabinet supporting a dated-looking sound system. The wall opposite is featureless, but upstage is a large cabinet containing various drinks bottles, glasses and various knick-knacks. Extreme downstage is a small glass fronted cabinet filled with ancient books. On top of this is a small table lamp and, piled haphazardly, several more battered books. On the back wall, R, is an upright piano which has obviously been used for many years. Piles of books, sheet music, etc., are stacked on top of this. A box piano stool is tucked beneath the closed keyboard. To the L of the piano, and almost by the door, is a large bookcase crammed with ancient tomes. On top of this, a hideous vase filled with fresh flowers. C of the room is a comfortable looking settee. Behind the settee is a narrow table on which the telephone stands L. It is also host to various ornaments. In front of the settee is a long coffee table. Several books occupy the R side of this and an open box of chocolates is displayed. Slightly below the settee, and flanking it L and R, are two armchairs. Both are angled C front as though facing the room's fireplace. The carpet, though of good quality once, is now somewhat threadbare. Various framed pictures decorate the walls. The light switch is L of the door and operates the central light

*When the scene begins, it is daylight, the room is empty and the
telephone is ringing. After a moment, Ida's voice is heard off* L

Ida (*off*) All right. All right. Hold your horses.

*She bustles into the room, hastily stuffing a duster into the pocket of the
faded overall she wears over her dress. She is in her early sixties and an
inveterate gossip*

(*Snatching up the phone and assuming a telephone voice*) Vicarage
speaking. ... That's right. Athelston vicarage. (*Forgetting the
unnatural voice*) Is it him you're wanting or Mrs Summerfield? Not that
it matters much. They're both out. (*Brightly*) But I can take a message
if you'd like? (*Warmly*) I'm Ida Cornish. Their cleaner. (*Proudly*)
Every Tuesday and Friday for the past four months and never missed
once. ... Yes. I know it's Wednesday, but somebody's coming to stay,
so I'm giving them extra time. Now do you want to leave a message
or are you calling back later? I've a bedroom to finish before he gets
here. ... Oh. I see. (*Curiously*) And where are you calling from? ...
Staffordshire. (*Chuckling*) I should have guessed, shouldn't I? I knew
you couldn't be local. Not with that accent. (*Smugly*) I've a good ear
for accents. Always have had. Should have been an actress, according
to my late husband, but you can't be doing with that sort of thing
when you've a family to look after, can you? (*Proudly*) Two daughters
in London, and a son in New Zealand. None of them married, but
they've all got partners and Mary's expecting in June, so that'll be
nice. There's one in the village, though. An actress, that is. Runs the
tea-room on Castle Street. (*Confidentially*) Never made a name for
herself. Just a walk-on in *Last of the Summer Wine* and a few lines in
Heartbeat. (*Shrugs*) It's why she gave up, I suppose. Though she does
make a good sponge cake. You've got to give her that much. There's
some I could name who couldn't do a decent sponge to save their
lives. (*Lowering her voice*) But I'm not impressed with her lemon
meringues. Too much crust and not enough lemon, for my taste.

Sheila (*calling, off* L) Are you there, Ida?

Ida (*turning and calling*) Through here, Sheila. (*Into the phone*) Sheila
Pashley. One of the neighbours.

*Sheila Pashley bustles into the room bursting with excitement. She is a
thick-set woman in her sixties, wearing a two piece suit, white blouse,
flat shoes and a heavy-looking bead necklace*

Sheila (*blurting it out*) I've just heard the news. From Molly Fisher at
the Spar shop. (*Seeing Ida on the phone*) Sorry. (*She hastily covers
her mouth*)

Ida (*into the phone*) I'll tell them you called, anyway. Bye. (*She replaces the receiver*)

Sheila (*embarrassed*) I didn't know you were on the phone. Nothing important, was it?

Ida (*shaking her head*) Just a wrong number. So what news is this, then? Not Tony Morrison again? 'Cause if it is, you needn't believe a word of it. I saw him outside the Post Office only an hour ago and there wasn't a mark on him.

Sheila (*impatiently*) No, no. It's nothing to do with Tony Morrison. (*Eyes sparkling*) It's Brandon Walsh.

Ida (*blankly*) Who?

Sheila (*excitedly*) This visitor they're expecting.

Ida still looks blank

(*Impatiently*) Don't say you've never heard of him. He wrote that thing on television. The one you raved about last month. (*Prompting*) The missing postman.

Ida (*dismissively*) You can't have that right. What would he be doing here?

Sheila (*sitting on the settee; confidentially*) According to Amy Ferris— who heard it from Gladys Appleton and told Molly—he went to the same school as Reverend Summerfield. And Lydia Summerfield's his cousin on his stepmother's side.

Ida (*scornfully*) And how'd Gladys Appleton know that? She couldn't give you the name of her own father with any certainty. (*She pulls the duster out of her pocket*)

Sheila (*beaming*) She heard them discussing it with Henry Wilson while she was doing the brasses. You know how voices carry at that end of the church? (*Pointedly*) Remember Tom Silver and the butcher's wife? (*Eagerly*) So what do you think?

Ida (*flatly*) About what? (*She flicks her duster at the telephone*)

Sheila Brandon Walsh, of course.

Ida (*pretending indifference*) I don't think anything. (*Tightly*) Except if Amy Ferris has anything to do with it, it'll be all round the village by the time he gets here. (*Annoyed*) It's scandalous the way some folk can't keep their noses out of other people's business.

Sheila (*squirming slightly*) Well, you must admit, he'll be a breath of fresh air in this place. It's not every day we get somebody famous here.

Ida (*sniffily*) I'd hardly call him famous on the strength of a television play.

Sheila (*correcting her*) But he's written books, as well, Ida. Six of them.

I asked at the library and she looked them up on the Internet. (*Coyly*) I've put an order in for his last one. (*Quoting*) "The Truth Behind the Edgemoor Mystery."

Ida (*surprised*) Since when did you start reading murder mysteries?

Sheila It's not a murder mystery. It's factual. About the Edgemoor Cross affair in 1765.

Ida Never heard of it.

Sheila (*pityingly*) Well, of course you haven't. That's what it's about. (*Lowering her voice*) It was all covered up, according to him. (*Confidentially*) A Government conspiracy to protect George the Third.

Ida (*dryly*) I bet that was a best-seller. (*She heads for the door*)

Sheila (*startled*) Where are you going?

Ida (*halting*) To put the kettle on. I presume you'll not say "no" to a cup of tea and a biscuit?

Sheila (*puzzled*) Well, no. But won't they mind?

Ida (*patiently*) They'll not be back till after I've gone, and a couple of cups of tea's not likely to plunge 'em into bankruptcy, is it?

Sheila (*curious*) So where are they, then? It's not often they're out together, is it? She seems to spend half her time in London.

Ida They've gone to Norwich to pick their visitor up. Left before I got here.

Sheila (*puzzled*) So how did you get in?

Ida (*dryly*) How do you think? They'd not bolted the cat-flap. (*Relenting*) I've got my own keys in case of emergencies. (*Impatiently*) Now, do you want that tea or don't you?

Without waiting for an answer, she exits and turns R

Sheila (*after a moment*) Who's been rattling her cage? (*Knowingly*) Jealous because she's not the first to know, I expect. (*Smugly*) Well, wait till she hears my other bit of news. That'll wipe the smile off her face. (*She leans back with a satisfied smirk on her lips*)

A moment or two later, Ida enters with a tray of tea things

Ida (*flatly*) Be ready in a minute or two. (*She moves down to the coffee table*)

Sheila (*sitting up again*) You don't know how long he's staying, do you?

Ida (*still put out*) Who?

Sheila Brandon Walsh.

Ida (*in mock surprise*) Oh—didn't she mention it? (*She deposits the tray*) I'm surprised you've not got his shoe size and how much he carries in his wallet. Must be losing her grip, Amy Ferris. (*Affecting disinterest*) And what else did she tell you?

Sheila (*shrugging*) Nothing, really— (*Slyly*) Except he was here to write a book.

Ida (*frowning*) Book?

Sheila (*blurting it out*) About the Lilywhite murder.

Ida (*after staring at her for a moment*) I'll get that tea.

She hurries out

Sheila (*to herself in satisfaction*) I knew that'd shake her. (*Singing softly, but gleefully*) "Two, two, the Lilywhite boys...Clothèd all in green, O-O... One is one and all alone... And evermore shall be so."

There are a few moments of silence

Ida re-enters carrying a teapot

Ida (*flatly*) Better make this quick. (*She moves down to the settee*) I've no time for gossip this morning. (*She sits next to Sheila and pours the tea*) Some of us have work to do.

Sheila (*thoughtfully*) Makes you wonder, doesn't it? I mean—who'd be interested in that? He wasn't exactly Leonardo di Cuppachino, was he? If they've not found out who did it after this time, what good's a book going to do?

Ida (*tartly*) It's all her doing, if you ask my opinion. (*Handing Sheila a cup and saucer*) Gwendoline Cranshawe. She'll not be satisfied till somebody's life's in ruins.

Sheila (*doubtfully*) Well— you know more than me about it, but I can't see how she'd be involved. Not after all the fuss. I'm surprised she's still here. If I'd found myself in her shoes, I'd have been off like a shot. (*She sips at her tea*)

Ida (*snorting*) And so would anyone else with a scrap of decency. She's got a mind like a sewer, that one. (*Hotly*) She'd not have accused any of mine and got away with it, I can tell you.

Sheila (*frowning*) But if she did see them in the quarry—and heard what she said they said——?

Ida (*sharply*) It was all lies. I've told you before. She had her knife into those two from the day they came here. You know how much she wanted that tea-room—and they snatched it from under her nose before she had time to find her gold-plated cheque book. (*Seething*) It was bad enough he was murdered in the first place, but to tell the police his brother killed him—well—the mind boggles. (*She angrily sips at her tea*)

Sheila (*uncomfortably*) She didn't exactly say he'd done it, Ida.

Ida (*indignantly*) She might as well have. I shudder to think what that couple went through before the police found out they were barking up the wrong tree. And now she's at it again.

Sheila (*agog*) You don't think it was her asked Brandon Walsh to write this book about it, do you?

Ida Well, nobody else would. If the police think some foreigner shot him, then that should be the end of it. We don't need it all raked up again. Especially by somebody who thinks——

The door chimes sound and they both react

(*To Sheila; flustered*) Finish your tea.

Ida puts down her cup, gets to her feet and bustles out into the hall, L

Sheila hastily gulps her tea, puts down the cup and saucer, and rises

Ida (*off* L; *surprised*) David.

David (*off* L; *angrily*) Where's Eddie Summerfield?

Ida (*off* L; *flustered*) He's not in.

David (*off* L; *raging*) Then I'll wait till he's back. I'm not having this.

David Lilywhite enters the room. He is a good-looking man in his forties, dressed in jacket, open necked shirt and light chinos

Ida hurries in after him

I'm not having it. (*Turning to Ida*) Is it true? He's coming here to write a book about us?

Ida (*soothingly*) We don't really know that.

David (*ignoring her*) It's all round the bloody village. Is he out of his mind? It was bad enough the first time round, but to have some tin-pot bloody writer grubbing about when we've finally managed to put it all behind us—it's not on. (*He notices Sheila for the first time and looks embarrassed*) Oh. Sorry, Mrs P. Didn't know you were here. I'm a bit upset. I can't believe he'd be so—so—insensitive.

Sheila (*soothingly*) I know just how you feel, David. I've only just heard about it myself. You must feel devastated.

David (*incredulously*) Devastated? I'm bloody furious. God knows what effect it'll have on Helen when she finds out. (*Despairingly*) I can't believe this is happening.

Ida (*kindly*) You mustn't take it to heart, love. It could all be a storm in a teacup. You know what this place is like. Some folks are never happier than when they're spreading gossip. (*She indicates the settee*) Now, why don't you sit down and let me get you a nice cup of tea?

David (*moving to the settee and sitting*) It's not as if we're public enemy number one, is it? I mean—we've done our best to fit in. We don't overcharge. Helen does the flowers on a Wednesday and I help out with the Hall twice a week. Why is he doing this?

Sheila (*lightly*) I'm sure there's an explanation. I mean—we don't even know if it's true yet, do we? And like I was saying to Ida, who'd be interested in a book about somebody getting shot for running a time-share swindle? (*She suddenly realises what she has said and looks aghast*)

David (*heavily*) It's all right, Sheila. I've heard it all before. (*More controlled*) He was involved in the Bonneville Scandal—and he did do time in jail for it. But he was my brother, jailbird or not, and I loved him. (*Acidly*) Though not in the way the Cranshawe woman seemed to think. Every time I see her, I want to vomit.

Ida (*primly*) The less said about that one, the better. Makes you ashamed to be a woman. I never did have much time for her, but after the things she said— well. If I see her coming my way, I cross the street to avoid her.

David (*grimly*) She never sets foot in our place.

Sheila (*stoutly*) I should think not, indeed. I wouldn't be seen dead in the same room as her—no matter how much I love Helen's Black Forest. (*She smiles warmly*)

David (*forcing a smile*) She does make a good cake, doesn't she?

Ida (*sensing the crisis is past*) I'll get you that tea.

David No thanks, Ida. I'll just wait for Summerfield to get back. I won't get in your way. I expect you've got work to do?

Ida (*diffidently*) Just the spare bedroom and a quick dust round in here. It won't take me long. I'm due at the Lawsons in half an hour.

Sheila (*brightly*) If you'd like a bit of company, David?

Ida (*firmly*) I thought you were late for your dental appointment?

Sheila stares at her in bewilderment

(*Sweetly*) Or was it your bunions? (*To David*) If she didn't have me to remind her, she'd forget her own head. (*To Sheila*) I'll see you out. (*She tilts her head as an indication for her to leave*)

Sheila (*reluctantly*) I'll—er—see you later, then. (*Smiling regretfully at David*)

Sheila moves to the door, Ida close behind, and they exit into the hall, L

David puts his head into his hands, dejectedly

   A moment or two later, Ida reappears

Ida (*confidentially*) She's my best friend, Sheila Pashley, but she must have invented the word gossip. (*She moves down to* R *of the settee*) I've told her to say nothing about you being here, so you don't need to worry about it getting round.

David (*looking up*) I don't give a damn who knows I'm here. I just want to find out what Summerfield thinks he's playing at. Haven't we gone through enough?

Ida (*staunchly*) I quite agree, David. But as you know, I never listen to gossip. (*Primly*) "Get the facts before you commit yourself," I've always said and, to tell you the truth, I've only heard the barest outline up to now. (*Prompting*) So—er?

David (*scowling*) I heard it from Molly Fisher when I popped in for The Courier. They've asked this hack to come up from London and do a book about Jason's murder. I ask you, what's it to do with the Summerfields? They weren't even living here when the bastard shot him. They'd never set eyes on him.

Ida (*frowning*) Does seem a bit strange, doesn't it?

David (*annoyed*) Strange? It's bloody bizarre. They couldn't possibly have any interest in him. He'd been living in Spain for ten years before he got arrested. Did the next five in jail, and only came out a few weeks before we came down here and took the tea-room. Two days later he was dead.

Ida (*shuddering*) We couldn't believe it, when we heard. None of us could. And it must have been terrible for you, not knowing anybody.

David (*distractedly*) She still has nightmares about it. Waking up in the middle of the night, with a madman aiming his shotgun at us.

Ida And if poor Jason hadn't come home late...

David It might have been me.

Ida (*hastily*) Now, you mustn't go thinking that, love. It was Jason he was looking for. They said so, didn't they? The police. Somebody he'd swindled.

David (*hotly*) But he couldn't have known I wasn't Jason, could he? The lights were out, and we looked like twins even though we weren't. He was three years older than me.

Ida (*reassuringly*) Good job Henry Wilson was passing and heard the shot. He was calling the police on his mobile when whoever it was ran out.

David I owe him my life. If it hadn't been for him, they'd have done me for the murder after what the Cranshawe bitch told them.

Ida (*soothingly*) Yes. But nobody believed it. You might get that kind of thing in London, but not round here. It's not natural, is it? Especially with your own brother. I've said it before and I'll say it again. She's got a mind like a sewer, that one. I'm surprised you didn't sue her.

David (*bitterly*) Believe you me—I thought about it. But the state Helen was in... (*His voice tails away*)

Ida (*kindly*) Well...it's all in the past, isn't it? And I can't see anybody beating down doors to read about something like that. I mean—no offence...but it's hardly Agatha Christie, is it? I should let him get on with it. He'll be lucky to sell a dozen.

Helen Lilywhite hurries into the room. She is an attractive woman in her forties, wearing a skirt and blouse, and has an anxious look on her face

Helen (*breathlessly*) Leave it, David. Let them... (*She realizes the expected argument is not taking place, and stops in her tracks*)

David (*turning his head to her*) Helen. What are you doing here? (*He rises and moves round to her*)

Helen (*shakily*) I heard you were heading in this direction.

David (*ruefully*) And came to stop me making a scene? (*Shaking his head*) You needn't have worried. They're not in. Poor Ida got the worst of it.

Ida looks embarrassed

So how'd you find out?

Helen (*grimacing*) It didn't take a genius. It was all they could talk about once Gladys had shown her face. Then when I heard you'd stormed out of Molly's place, I just had to come after you.

David (*frowning*) But what about the tea-room?

Helen (*reassuringly*) It's quite safe. Annie Milton's there.

David (*reluctantly*) We'd better get back. I'll speak to the Summerfields later.

Helen Just leave it, David. It's not as though we've anything to hide. If he wants to write his book, let him.

David (*protesting*) But what about Jason?

Helen (*firmly*) Whatever he did is on public record. It's nothing to do with us. We can't be held responsible.

Ida (*to Helen*) Exactly what I said, Helen.

David (*to Helen; stung*) So you're quite happy to have it dragged up again, are you? All the lies and gossip? Every personal detail exposed to public gaze? What if he interviews the Cranshawe woman? Do you think he wouldn't use her story?

Helen (*soothingly*) It wouldn't matter if he did. It'd just make her look a bigger fool than she was at the time.

David (*scowling*) Maybe it would. But you know what they say? "There's no smoke without fire". And we've a business to run.

Helen If I thought for a minute our trade would be affected, I'd be right behind you. But it's four years, now. Everybody knows us, and the idea that a book's going to make any difference is just—(*floundering for a word*)—stupid. There's nothing to worry about.

Ida (*firmly*) Quite right, love. If he comes round asking me questions, he'll get more than he's bargained for. And that goes for any of the others. There'll not a word be said against you by anybody in Athelston.

David (*to Helen; shamefacedly*) We'd better be going. (*To Ida*) Don't bother the Summerfields, Ida. Forget I was even here.

Ida (*warmly*) You're welcome any time.

David and Helen exit

The minute they have gone, Ida hurries to the telephone and dials

(*Into the phone*) Is that Chloris? It's Mrs Cornish. Is your mother in? I'd just like a quick word if she has a minute. (*Disappointed*) Oh. Just gone out. Well, do you know where? ... Oh. (*With forced brightness*) Well, never mind, dear. It was nothing important. (*Breaks the connection*) I wonder if Brenda's home? (*She begins to dial hastily*)

Roy Steadman appears at the french windows. He is a surly-looking man in his mid forties, dressed in gardening clothes

Seeing Ida, he taps on the glass. Startled, she turns to face him and quickly replaces the receiver

(*Sharply*) What do you want?

He gestures for her to open the windows and she does so with bad grace

Roy (*entering*) Back door's locked.

Ida So?

Roy I need the shed key.

Ida What for?

Roy (*sarcastically*) We're having a dinner and dance in there and I need to set the tables and chairs. (*Harshly*) What do you think I want it for? It's Wednesday, isn't it? The lawn needs cutting.

Ida (*tartly*) You'd better wait there. I'll see if I can find it for you. You're not bringing soil in all over the carpet. It's bad enough as it is. (*She makes for the door*)

Roy If you open the back door, I'll get it myself.

Ida (*pausing*) Not while I'm in charge, Roy Steadman. If anything goes missing, it'll be me they'll hold responsible, not you.

She exits

Roy (*stepping further inside and calling after her*) You can put the kettle on while you're at it. I always get coffee from Mrs S.

He stands for a moment, then fumbles in his pocket for his mobile. Punching in the numbers, he puts it to his ear and lowers his voice

Mark? Roy Steadman. Running a bit late, but I'll be there before dark. We are still on for tonight, aren't we? ... Just checking. ... (*Frowning*) I thought you had one of your own? ...So what happened to it? ... Doesn't matter. I'll bring mine. Nobody knows I have it, so it won't be a problem. Just don't let on.

Voices are heard in the hall, and he hastily ends the call, replacing the phone in his pocket

Lydia (*off* L)...And the next thing he knew, he was knee deep in it. (*She laughs*)

Edwin (*off; amused*) That's not strictly true, Lydia. If he hadn't been looking...

Lydia Summerfield enters the room. She is an attractive woman in her thirties, wearing a summer dress, high-heeled shoes and carrying a handbag

Lydia sees Roy

...at you in those sexy shorts and indecent top, it never would have happened.

Lydia (*slightly puzzled*) Mr Steadman.

Brandon (*off*) So even a Bishop's not immune to hidden charms?

Edwin (*off*) There wasn't much hidden, I can tell you.

The two men laugh

Lydia (*calling hastily*) Visitor.

Roy (*easily*) Called for the shed key. She's just sorting it out for me.

Edwin Summerfield enters. He is a pleasant man in his late thirties, wearing slacks, clerical grey shirt and collar and black shoes. He is followed by Brandon Walsh who is also in his thirties, wearing chinos, open-necked shirt and loafers

Edwin Roy? (*Puzzled*) What are you doing here?
Roy It's Wednesday morning.
Edwin But—didn't you get my message?

Roy looks puzzled

From Henry? I asked him to tell you. (*Shaking his head*) Obviously not. It's just that the kitchen fitters cancelled yesterday, so we've had to stack the new units in the shed till next Tuesday, and the mower's underneath them at the back. It doesn't look too bad, the old lawn, so I think we can give it a miss this week.
Roy (*not too happily*) Fine by me. But I set this morning aside.
Edwin (*hastily*) I know. I know. But don't worry. We'll come to some arrangement. Wouldn't want to see you out of pocket.
Roy Better be off, then. Take the chance to tidy my own patch. You know what they say, Vicar? The cobbler's son is always the worst shod.
Lydia (*brightly*) We'll see you next week, then?

Roy nods and exits through the french windows

Lydia gives a small sigh of relief and beams at the others

Now, who's for a nice cup of tea?
Brandon I'd rather a cold lager.
Lydia (*raising an eyebrow*) It's good to know you haven't changed. Once a drunk, always a drunk.
Edwin I wouldn't mind a lager, myself, actually.
Lydia (*shaking her head in amusement*) Two lagers coming up.

Lydia exits to R

Brandon (*glancing around*) So this is Athelston.
Edwin (*indicating the armchair* R) Sit down. Take the weight off your feet.

Brandon moves to the armchair and sits

Yes. This is Athelston. (*Sitting on the settee*) Not exactly what I was hoping for when I took the living, but better than the other option. Couldn't see myself as an inner city man, being a country boy, but apart from the usual problems, we're not doing too badly.

Brandon Decent congregation?

Edwin On High Days and holidays. Much the same as everywhere else. Christenings are up, but I've only done a handful of weddings since we came here.

Brandon And what about funerals?

Edwin (*shaking his head*) They're long lived in these parts. They had to shoot somebody to start a cemetery. (*He realizes what he has said and looks abashed*) Sorry. Didn't mean to say that. Bit insensitive.

Brandon I won't rat on you. But it does remind me why you wanted me down here.

Edwin It was Lydia's idea, actually. Thought it might be up your street.

Brandon (*grimacing*) Not the thing I usually tackle. I'm more your historical "cover-up" writer. (*Hastily*) But I'm always on the lookout for interesting ideas. Refresh my memory.

Edwin Well... it was a couple of years before we came here. There'd been a bit of a falling out between one of the parishioners and the couple who'd bought the local tea-room, David and Helen Lilywhite. Nice pair—we'll take you down to meet them while you're here—but they'd brought his brother with them, too. Nobody knew it then, of course, but he'd just come out of jail. Some kind of property swindle abroad. Anyway... about two days after they got here, they woke to find an intruder in the bedroom, pointing a shotgun at them. Just as he was going to pull the trigger, the brother turned up and he panicked. Gave him both barrels and took off like a greyhound. The verger spotted him haring up the street and called the police, but by the time they got there, Jason—the brother—was dead and the killer was long gone.

Brandon So what had this Crayshaw woman to do with it?

Edwin Cranshawe. Gwendoline Cranshawe. Well—she was the one who'd had the barney with the Lilywhites, and told the police she'd seen the boys in the old quarry that same afternoon (*uncomfortably*)— having sex. (*Hastily*) There wasn't a grain of truth in it, of course. Jack Middlemarch—my predecessor—swore David was as straight as a die. He'd known him from way back and was the main reason the Lilywhites moved here from Lincoln. But the police swallowed it, and wasted days trying to prove David and Jason weren't brothers, but lovers, and Helen Lilywhite had a complete and utter breakdown.

Brandon (*puzzled*) But there were witnesses, you said?

Edwin (*nodding*) Henry Wilson—our verger, and Helen Lilywhite, of course. But Henry's known to the police—a little drink problem—and a wife's not exactly regarded as impartial, so it was all quite messy until they started digging into Jason's background. Then it all fell into place. He'd ripped off quite a few people in his heyday, and more than one had threatened to kill him. Obviously somebody followed him down here, broke into the house and shot him. If he'd waited a few more weeks, he could have saved himself the trouble. According to the coroner, Jason had terminal cancer.

Brandon So what happened then?

Edwin As far as I know... nothing. They never caught anybody. Wasn't even a suspect. And they never even found the weapon.

Brandon So it's still an open case?

Edwin I suppose so. Which is why Lydia thought you might be interested.

Lydia enters with a tray holding two glasses of lager and one of lemonade

Lydia (*as she enters*) Interested in what?

Brandon (*looking up*) The Lilywhite thing. We were just doing a re-cap.

Lydia (*depositing the tray on the table behind the settee*) Give yourself time to settle in. We've hardly got our coats off. (*Handing Brandon a glass*) Besides—I'm the one who asked you down here. It's me you should be grilling, not old sober-sides. (*Handing Edwin his glass*)

Edwin (*lightly*) Not so sober with this inside me. (*Tipping his glass*) Cheers.

They all raise their drinks

Brandon (*after gulping a mouthful*) So what do you think I can do?

Lydia You can go upstairs and unpack your case. Ida's finished your room, so you can freshen up before we bundle you off to the *Plough* for a nice leisurely lunch.

Brandon Can't we have something here?

Edwin Not if you value your life. Lydia's cooking is not her finest asset. More often than not, it's a case of cordoned off, rather than cordon bleu.

Lydia (*lightly slapping the back of his head*) Pig. (*Haughtily*) I do a rather amazing shepherd's pie when I put my mind to it. Even the bishop says he's never tasted anything like it.

The two men laugh

What? (*Puzzled*) What?

Edwin (*to Brandon*) We can knock up a few sandwiches if you really don't fancy the *Plough*. But you'll be missing a treat. They've quite a reputation in this place, the Walker family. Father trained under some famous French chef, and the eldest daughter's running her own place in New York. (*He drinks*)

Lydia Not that we've been there, of course. But hope springs eternal.

Brandon Well, how about me taking you for a bite? We could go there tonight. To the *Plough*, I mean. Not New York.

Lydia (*quickly*) We'd love it. It's weeks since we had a decent night out. But not tonight. I spent half my housekeeping on a joint of beef and a bottle of plonk, and there's veg straight from the garden with strawberry flan for desert. (*Anxiously*) You do like chard, don't you?

Edwin She means the leaf...not the roast. (*Grinning*) Though you may not notice the difference.

Brandon (*lightly*) One of these days, she's going to brain you with a very heavy frying pan. (*To Lydia*) Haven't a clue what chard is, darling, but I'll try anything once. And I'm sure it'll taste like heaven.

Lydia (*to Edwin; snootily*) You see? There are still some gentlemen left in the world. (*To Brandon; sweetly*) I'll give you a double helping. (*Sipping at her lemonade*)

The door chimes sound

Edwin (*rising*) I'll get it.

Lydia No, no. I'm closest. (*Putting her glass down*) You look after my adoring fan.

She exits and turns L

Brandon (*grinning*) I don't know about adoring, but I'm still a dab hand at buttering up. Is she really as bad a cook as she was?

Edwin She does try, bless her. Even had Maurice Walker give her a few lessons, but it's a lost cause. Do most of the cooking myself these days. Nothing fancy, though. I'm no Gordon Ramsay.

Brandon Me neither. Eat out, mainly. When I remember. Once I'm into a book, food's the last thing I'm thinking about.

Lydia re-enters, followed by a grim-looking Maurice Walker. He is in his fifties, slim and has a small moustache

Lydia (*uneasily*) It's Maurice.

Edwin (*rising*) Maurice. (*He moves round the settee and holds out his hand*)

Maurice ignores it and looks pointedly at Brandon

(*Realizing*) Oh—er—Brandon Walsh. Lydia's cousin. He's staying with us for a week or two.

Maurice (*coldly*) So I've heard. (*To Brandon*) Some kind of writer, aren't you?

Brandon (*modestly*) Just the odd book or two. And a bit of television work.

Maurice (*harshly*) And you think that gives you the right to go digging into other people's lives, do you? Making your wild accusations and dragging their names through the mud?

Brandon (*taken aback*) I'm sorry?

Maurice Not half as sorry as you will be if you start printing your filthy lies about people whose boots you're not even fit to lick.

Edwin (*protesting*) Maurice...

Maurice (*ignoring him*) Take my word, Mr Walsh. You're not wanted in Athelston. Point your grubby finger in their direction, and you'll have me to reckon with. Understand?

Brandon (*rising*) Look. There seems to be some sort of——

Maurice (*cutting in*) I said, do you understand? One word and it'll be the last you ever write. And before you ask... no, it's not a threat. It's a promise. (*To Edwin and Lydia; scornfully*) I'd have thought you'd have had more sense than to instigate this...witch-hunt. Do you know what that couple went through five years ago? Do you realize the damage you could be causing? (*Bitterly*) No. I don't suppose you do. (*Harshly*) She nearly killed herself, that woman. And he lost his brother. (*Scornfully*) You haven't the sense you were born with. (*He turns to exit*)

Lydia (*quickly*) Maurice. Listen to me. I don't know what you've heard, but you've got it all wrong. Brandon's not here to make accusations. We want him to find out the truth.

Maurice (*turning back to her*) And what truth's that, then? (*Grimly*) Whoever shot Jason Lilywhite deserves a medal. He was scum, that man, and the world's a better place without him. If I'd known what I know now, I'd have killed the bastard myself.

Edwin (*soothingly*) Look. Why don't you sit down and listen——

Maurice (*bluntly*) I've done all the listening I want to do, Vicar. You'll not see me again till he's back under whatever stone he came out from.

Lydia (*protesting*) You're blowing this out of proportion, Maurice. (*Soothingly*) Look...we'll book a table for tomorrow and have a——
Maurice (*bluntly*) No, you won't. You're not welcome in my establishment. And by the way, the Apostles'll be needing another organist. Our Phillip's just resigned.

Maurice exits

Brandon (*astounded*) My God. Neanderthal rules.
Edwin (*embarrassed*) Sorry about that. He's not usually——
Brandon No, no. It's not your fault.
Edwin I can't think how the news got round so quickly.
Lydia (*wryly*) Well, that puts paid to the book idea.
Brandon (*thoughtfully*) Does it? Quite the opposite in my opinion. (*He sits again*) Go over it again for me, will you?

The others stare at him as the lights fade to Black-out

Scene 2

The following Tuesday. The glasses and tea things have been cleared away, the box of chocolates has been removed and fresh flowers are in the vase. Books and magazines have been moved to different locations, but otherwise, the room is unchanged. The french windows are open, but the door is closed

It is late morning and Edwin sits on the settee reading a battered-looking book and occasionally making notes on an A4 pad resting on the coffee table. After a few moments, the door opens and a distant hammering can be heard. Ida bustles in, carrying a tray on which rests a mug of coffee and a doughnut on a small plate

Ida (*moving down to him*) Brought you a coffee and doughnut. (*Sourly*) Best I could manage with that going on.
Edwin (*smiling*) Thanks, Ida. How're they doing? (*Putting the book down beside him on the settee*)
Ida (*putting the tray on the coffee table*) Not as well as I'd prefer. You'll not be cooking tonight's dinner in there, I can tell you. You'll be lucky if it's ready by tomorrow.

The hammering stops

Edwin (*philosophically*) Looks like a take-away, then. And as we're not very welcome at the *Plough*, it'll have to be the Lotus Garden.
Ida (*looking at him askance*) Do you like Chinese food, then?
Edwin (*picking up his coffee*) Now and again. Yes.
Ida (*shuddering*) Never touch the stuff, myself.

The hammering starts again

A nice pork chop, or chicken casserole's my favourite. (*Suddenly*) Why don't I do you one of those? I could bring it across from my place whenever you're ready?
Edwin (*embarrassed*) Very kind of you, Ida, but—
Ida I'm not a bad cook, you know.
Edwin (*hastily*) I'm sure you're not. But we couldn't possibly—
Ida It's no trouble. And I hate cooking for myself, these days. It's not the same without the kids eating me out of house and home every mealtime.
Edwin Well… If you're sure you don't mind?
Ida (*beaming*) All settled, then. As soon as I've finished the dining-room, I'll go down to Bransom's for a nice fresh chicken. You can settle up with me later.

She exits happily, closing the door behind her

The hammering stops

Edwin takes a bite of the doughnut and sips his coffee. The telephone rings. Quickly putting his doughnut down, he licks the sugar off his fingers before reaching over the back of the settee and picking up the receiver

Edwin Summerfield. Oh, good morning, Miss Cranshawe. …Well, yes. Of course. Is it something—er—? … No. No. Of course not. But he's—er— not here at present. Been in Lincoln since Friday. … Oh, yes. Yes. Any time now, I expect. I had a call about an hour ago. But if you could give me some idea of what… … Right. Right. (*Resigned*) I'll… er… mention it to him the minute he arrives. (*He takes the receiver from his ear and frowns at it before replacing it on the stand*)

The door opens again and Ida appears

Ida (*flatly*) The fat fellow wants a word with you. Something to do with the cooker point.

Edwin (*frowning*) Can't Lydia deal with it?

Ida She's gone to the Spar shop for milk. That's two pints they've got through since starting— and a pack of digestives. (*Tartly*) They'd not be getting it at my place, I can tell you. Not at the price they charge for a few lumps of chip-board and a box or two of tiles. They'd buy their own.

Edwin (*resignedly*) I'll see what the problem is. (*He puts the mug down, and stands*)

Ida Problem is, they want other folk doing their jobs for them.

Edwin (*moving to the door*) Better safe than sorry.

He sidles past her and exits R

Ida is about to follow him when the door chimes sound

She vanishes L, *and a moment later, her voice is heard off*

Ida (*off*) Oh. It's you.

Sheila (*off*) Well, don't sound so pleased.

Ida (*off*) It's nothing to do with being pleased. I'm trying to get finished so I can do a bit of shopping. What do you want?

Sheila (*off*) Well, it's not to see you. I was wanting a word with Vicar.

Ida (*off*) You'd better come in then. But don't keep him long. He's trying to write his sermon.

Ida appears in the doorway and ushers Sheila into the room. Sheila carries a large shopping bag with a hardbacked book and a large manilla envelope inside it

You can wait in here. But don't touch anything. Sit in the armchair.

Ida exits R

Sheila sits in the armchair R *and waits. The hammering begins again and she winces*

A moment later, Edwin re-enters

Edwin (*smiling*) Mrs Pashley. (*He closes the door and the hammering stops*) Sorry about the noise. They're fitting the new kitchen. (*He moves to the settee*) What can I do for you?

Sheila (*hesitating*) Well—to be perfectly honest—it's Mr Walsh I wanted to see. (*Almost girlishly*) I got his book. (*Patting her bag*) From the library.

Edwin I see. (*He sits*)

Sheila And I was wondering—as he's staying with you—if he wouldn't mind giving me his autograph?

Edwin Well...I—er—I'm sure he wouldn't. But—a library book, you said? Isn't that—er—

Sheila (*hastily*) Oh, I didn't mean the book. (*She chuckles*) But his picture's on the back, so I had it photocopied in the Post Office. (*Proudly*) It'll go straight into my scrapbook with all the other cuttings. (*Confidentially*) About the Lilywhite murder. (*Beaming*) They're all in there. Everything the papers said. I could show it to Mr Walsh if he'd like? (*Anxiously*) He is going to write about it, isn't he?

Edwin (*uncomfortably*) It's difficult to say. He hasn't committed himself. Not with the family's objections.

Sheila (*fretfully*) But he must. How else are they going to solve it? The police aren't doing anything to catch him.

Edwin (*reasonably*) He could be anywhere by now. He didn't leave a trace. If Henry hadn't spotted him coming out of the cottage, who'd have believed the Lilywhites?

Sheila Well, he wasn't the only witness, was he? Roy Steadman saw him.

Edwin (*surprised*) Roy?

Sheila Not that he told the police. He'd not help them with anything after they'd had him locked up for throwing stones at young Mr Prentice. He'd closed the quarry down, you see, and there was a lot of bitterness. Most of the others found work, but not Roy. He didn't have a job for years. That's why he took up gardening with poaching as a sideline. You can't live on benefits. But he saw him, all right. Couldn't have missed him.

Edwin (*curious*) Why's that?

Sheila Because the night it happened, I was sitting by my bedroom window for a breath of cool air, and Roy Steadman was hanging over Doris Jackson's gate, throwing his insides up. I could see him clear as day, under the street lamp. The minute we heard the shot, he stood up, staggered to the corner and set off down Castle Street as fast as he could.

Edwin Towards the tea-room.

Sheila Exactly. So if Henry Wilson saw the murderer running away, why didn't Roy Steadman? (*Smiling triumphantly*)

Edwin So—why didn't you tell the police this?

Sheila Well, I knew he hadn't anything to do with it. And they had got Henry's statement. It just puzzled me why he never said anything— even when the place was crawling with reporters. Some folks get thousands for stories like that.

Edwin You weren't tempted yourself?

Sheila (*shaking her head*) Let sleeping dogs lie's my motto. And besides, he's a bit of a temper, has Roy. I wouldn't want to get the wrong side of him.

Edwin Even so...

Sheila You've seen what it's like in this place, Vicar. Even Reverend Middlemarch knew not to upset certain people. (*Regretfully*) I can't believe he went just like that. The times he'd been up to that belfry. Must have known it like the back of his hand.

Edwin Truly tragic. But God's will, of course. And he was a trifle unsteady on his feet, according to Bishop Arthur.

Sheila If only he'd worn slip-ons. My George tripped on a shoelace once, and ended up in plaster for weeks. But to think of poor Reverend Middlemarch bouncing down those stone steps...

Edwin (*hastily*) Yes. Well, we needn't go into that.

Sheila We couldn't believe it. First Jason Lilywhite—then him. And only two days apart. (*Reassuringly*) But we're all glad you're here, Vicar. You do a lovely sermon. And so explicit. We'd no idea what real sin was till you came to Athelston.

Edwin (*nonplussed*) Thank you.

Sheila (*rising*) But I mustn't keep you. I know you're busy. But if you wouldn't mind giving this to Mr Walsh, (*taking the large manilla envelope from her bag*) I'd be very grateful. I'll collect it any time that's convenient.

Edwin (*rising*) I'll see you out. (*He takes the envelope*)

Sheila (*brightly*) No, no. I know the way.

Sheila smiles and exits

Edwin closes the door and moves down to the table behind the settee. He puts down the envelope, moves round to the front of the settee and sits. Picking up his mug, he takes a sip of coffee, pulls a face and puts the mug down again. Picking up his book, he scans it briefly, then picks up his pen to write a note. Before he can do so, he pauses and frowns

Edwin Roy *Steadman.*

The door opens and Ida appears

Ida Was that her leaving, Vicar? I told her you were busy.

Edwin (*distractedly*) Yes. She's just gone.

Ida Right. Well I'd better be going myself. It's no use thinking about the hall and kitchen till that lot have finished. But give me a ring whenever you're ready and I'll be over with the casserole before you've time to set the table.

Edwin (*still preoccupied*) Thank you.

Ida turns to exit

(*Suddenly*) Ida...

She turns back

Mrs Pashley...(*He stops*)
Ida (*puzzled*) Yes?
Edwin (*hesitantly*) You've known her for some time?
Ida (*still puzzled*) Thirty years or so. Yes.
Edwin (*half embarrassed*) Then would you say that—well—any information she gave you—could safely be relied on?
Ida (*suspiciously*) Why? What's she been saying?
Edwin (*hastily*) Nothing. I mean—nothing important. It was just— she mentioned a bit of trouble at the quarry—a few years back.
Ida (*dismissively*) Oh, that. Storm in a teacup, in my opinion. We all knew it was closing a full year before Ted Prentice put the notice up. The only trouble came from hotheads like Barry Farmer and Roy Steadman. Soon as they put Steadman away for a few months, the other one made himself scarce. Good riddance to bad rubbish, I'd say.
Edwin So he really did go to jail? Roy Steadman, I mean.
Ida Oh, yes. Best thing that ever happened to him. By the time he came out, he'd got rid of the chip on his shoulder and found himself an honest job. (*Worried*) You're not thinking of sacking him, are you?
Edwin (*hastily*) No, no. Of course not. Wouldn't dream of it.
Ida (*mollified*) That's all right, then. I don't like him, I'll admit, but he's kept out of trouble ever since. And he's a good gardener. There's not a plant he doesn't know about.
Edwin (*lightly*) I'd better ask him to give Lydia some tips. She can't tell the difference between bluebells and asparagus.
Ida (*grudgingly*) Well, he's the one to do it. I'll give him that much. But I'd still keep an eye on the silver. (*Briskly*) Right. I'm off, then. And don't forget. Whenever you're ready.

She exits into the hall

Lydia (*off* L) You wouldn't believe the mess in Salmon Street. Of all the times to start digging the pavement up. Just off, Ida?

Ida (*off*) Nothing I can do in there. There's dust everywhere. I'll give it a good clean on Friday. (*Brightly*) But everything's fixed for tonight. You don't have to worry. You'll not go hungry. Bye.

Lydia appears in the doorway, carrying a large shopping bag, filled with goods

Lydia (*puzzled*) What was that about?

Edwin She's doing us a chicken casserole. (*Hastily*) I didn't ask. She volunteered.

Lydia (*protesting*) I've just bought this lot. Sliced ham, potato salad, coleslaw... and a tin of pears for dessert.

Edwin (*helplessly*) I couldn't turn her down, Lyd.

Lydia (*shrugging*) Oh, never mind. It won't get wasted. We can have it tomorrow. Is Brandon back yet?

Edwin Any time now, I expect. I told you he'd rung.

Lydia But that was over an hour ago. It's nearly lunch time. (*She sighs*) I'd better make more coffee. Keep the brutes happy. (*She turns to leave*)

Edwin (*grabbing his mug*) I wouldn't mind one myself, if you're at it. Never got a chance to finish this. (*He holds his mug out to her*)

The door chimes sound

I'll get it.

Edwin jumps to his feet, moves to the door, hands Lydia the mug and exits L. *Lydia exits and turns* R

(*Off; surprised*) Maurice.

Maurice (*off; gruffly*) Any chance of a minute or so?

Edwin (*off; uncertainly*) Of course. Come in.

A moment later Maurice appears in the doorway

Maurice (*entering*) Not disturbing anything, am I?

Edwin (*following him in*) No, no. Of course not. (*Warily*) Have a chair.

Maurice (*hesitantly*) I'll stand, if you don't mind.

There is a short silence as the two look at each other

Edwin (*gently*) Is there something I can do for you?

Maurice (*awkwardly*) It's more what I can do for you, Vicar. The thing is—(*blurting it out*) I've come to apologize. For what I said the other day. I wasn't thinking straight.

Edwin (*a little embarrassed*) Oh.

Maurice (*bitterly*) It's this place, you see? The village. I should be used to it by now. I've lived here all my life. But it still gets to me. All the gossip and backbiting. You don't know who to believe. Or what. Sometimes I just want to—(*he halts and struggles for control*) Well—like I said—I spoke out of turn and I'd no right to say what I did say. It was bad manners on my part and I hope you'll accept my apology.

Edwin (*relieved*) Of course.

Maurice (*awkwardly*) Well—I've said what I had to say, so I'll leave you in peace. And if ever you do fancy a meal at the *Plough*, you've only to say the word. We'll squeeze you in, somehow.

The hammering starts again and Maurice is slightly startled

Edwin (*apologetically*) Kitchen fitters. We're having a new one put in. It's a bit of a tip, at present.

Maurice (*relaxing a little*) Tell me about it. Three days it took for our Gina to get hers done. (*Suddenly*) Are you fixed for tonight, then?

The hammering stops

Edwin (*puzzled, then realising*) For a meal, you mean? Oh, yes. Yes. Ida's doing us a chicken casserole and bringing it over. (*Smiling*) We'd have come to the *Plough*, ordinarily.

Maurice (*abashed*) Yes. Well, as I said—you've only to say the word. (*Holding out his hand*) Friends again?

Edwin (*taking it*) Of course. We all fly off the handle from time to time. Clergy included.

They shake hands

(*Smiling*) I hear my predecessor had one or two off days.

Maurice Jack Middlemarch, you mean? (*Nodding*) Straight as a die, that man. No bowing and scraping with him. Said exactly what he thought and hang the consequences. None of that love thy neighbour nonsense with him. Wouldn't have her in here, even after Birdie retired. Cooked and cleaned for himself till the day he died.

Edwin (*frowning*) Wouldn't have who in here?

Maurice (*scowling*) Ida Cornish. Biggest gossip in the village. Apart from Sheila Pashley. (*Sourly*) Not that there's much to choose between those two and the rest of them. It's a bloody hotbed—sorry Vicar—in these parts. Got nothing better to do than tear other people's private lives to shreds and tatters for their own entertainment. (*Embarrassed*) It's why I got so het up when I heard that writer friend of yours had come down here to do a hatchet job on the Lilywhites.

Edwin (*protesting gently*) But he hadn't. There wasn't the slightest intention of——

Maurice I know... I spoke to Helen on Friday. He'd been in to see her.

Edwin (*surprised*) Really?

Maurice Explained everything. How you thought he might help put Jason's killer behind bars and give them both closure. Made me feel more of a prat than I am. I should have let him explain.

Edwin (*reassuringly*) Well... there's no harm done. And I'm glad we've had a chance to clear the air. (*Warmly*) Are you sure you won't sit down?

Maurice (*shaking his head*) Better be off. I've things to do for tonight. Big party in from Leeminster. (*Remembering*) Oh... (*He grimaces*) And I'm sorry about Sunday as well. The organ, I mean. It wasn't Phil's idea. I put him in a bad position.

Edwin (*easily*) All in the past. Lydia plays the piano, so we managed on the old harmonium. It'll be nice to see him back, though. (*Suddenly concerned*) He—er—he is coming back, isn't he?

Maurice (*nodding*) Be there Sunday morning.

Lydia enters with a mug of coffee and stops short when she sees Maurice

(*Embarrassed*) Lydia. (*He looks down at his feet*)

Lydia nods to him, warily

Edwin (*hastily*) He's just been apologizing for last week. Bit of a misunderstanding.

Lydia (*uncertainly*) Oh. (*She gives the mug to Edwin*)

Maurice (*looking up, shamefacedly*) I'd no right coming here with all my guns blazing. You're not like the rest of them in this place, and I should have known better. It won't happen again, I promise.

Lydia (*relieved*) Thank goodness for that. You were the first friend we had when we came to Athelston and the idea of us falling out was terrible. (*Impulsively*) Why don't you come for supper one night?

Edwin (*in mock alarm*) Steady on. We've only just made up our differences. We don't want to put him in hospital.

Lydia glowers at him

Maurice (*to Lydia*) Take no notice. Anybody who'll ladle tomato sauce on to deep-fried Stilton's no authority on cooking, in my opinion. I'd be happy to join you, any time.
Edwin (*protesting*) I like tomato sauce.
Lydia (*snootily*) So we'd noticed. (*Hissing*) Philistine.

Maurice grins. Edwin pretends to be offended and moves round to the front of the settee to sit

(*Linking arms with Maurice*) Well now we're on speaking terms again, you might be able to help with something.
Maurice What is it?
Lydia You can see the Memorial Hall from the *Plough's* kitchen, can't you?
Maurice (*nodding*) It's just across the road. Why?
Lydia (*grimacing*) I saw Mrs Vasey a few minutes ago. It seems they had a break-in, last night.

Edwin looks surprised

Maurice (*frowning*) First I've heard of it. Was anything damaged?
Lydia (*releasing his arm*) Only the under-stage door. They'd prised off the padlock to get inside.
Edwin (*frowning*) Is anything missing? (*Putting his mug on the coffee table*)
Lydia Not that they know of, but it's hard to say. Most of the stuff's been down there for years. Bits of old scenery, folding tables, a set of drums and half a rail of fancy dress costumes under a dust sheet. But she's called the police. To be on the safe side. They're coming over this afternoon. (*To Maurice*) I just wondered if you'd seen anything?
Maurice (*considering*) Nothing I can think of. (*Puzzled*) Who'd want to break into that place?
Edwin Probably teenagers. Three of them spray-painted the vestry window a few weeks back. Henry Wilson spotted them, but they were off before he was halfway up the path. All in their hoodies, or whatever you call them, so no chance of recognizing them.
Maurice (*shaking his head*) Used to have a youth club there, years back. And Scouts and Brownies. But nobody wants them, these days. Too interested in their mobile phones and computer games. Stan Patterson would turn in his grave.
Edwin (*frowning*) Patterson?

Maurice Before your time. Local musician. Ran the youth club jazz
band for donkey's years. Supplied all the instruments and trained the
kids. Used to pack the old hall on a Saturday night. Over eighty, he
was, and still played like Benny Goodman. (*Regretfully*) All fell apart
when he died, though. Most of his stuff's still under the stage. Nothing
much now to keep them off the streets.

Edwin (*protesting lightly*) We have tried.

Maurice I know. I'm not criticizing. Jack Middlemarch had the self
same problem. You can't get through to them. If you want your kids
to be happy, these days, you buy them anything that beeps, buzzes, or
bangs and avoid living in country villages with no public transport.

Lydia (*wryly*) That's one thing we'll never have to worry about.

Maurice There's still time.

Edwin (*shaking his head*) Not for us, I'm afraid. We can't have a family.
We lost our first and there were complications.

Maurice (*uncomfortable*) Oh. I'm sorry to hear it.

Lydia (*smiling brightly*) But we're happy enough with each other—even
though he is a philistine. So when can we expect you? For supper, that
is? (*Hopefully*) Sometime this week?

Maurice (*frowning*) I've parties in most nights.

Lydia looks disappointed

(*Smiling*) But if Dad'll hold the fort when I close the kitchen, I might
manage tomorrow.

Lydia (*brightening*) Wednesday it is, then.

Maurice Right. Well, I'd better be off. I'm glad we've straightened
things out. I'll try to watch my manners in future.

Lydia I'll see you out.

Maurice No need. I know where the door is.

Maurice exits and turns L

Edwin (*sighing with relief*) Well, that's one worry less for Sunday.
Phillip'll be playing the organ for us, so we needn't rely on that awful
harmonium again.

Lydia (*hurt*) I did the best I could.

Edwin (*hastily*) I know, darling. But the man who built that one must
have had a grudge against music. It was worse than bagpipes.

Lydia I thought you liked bagpipes?

Edwin Only in the wilds of Scotland. Not the middle of morning
service. I expected Robert the Bruce to come charging down the aisle
waving his sword. Not to mention Bonnie Prince Charlie and Flora
Macdonald.

Lydia And speaking of Flora, you do know the yew by the lych-gate needs looking at? It nearly took my eye out this morning. You might mention it to Roy. It does overhang the pavement, so it's our responsibility.

Edwin I'll make a note of it.

Brandon (*off* L) Anybody home?

They turn to look at Brandon as he enters. He is now in a jacket and trousers and carries an overnight bag and a set of car keys

Sorry I'm late. Traffic was heavier than I expected. But here I am. Safe and sound and bursting with all the information I was chasing. (*Putting the bag down*) Was that the demon chef I saw leaving just now?

Edwin The one and only...but I think we've exorcised him. He came round to apologize.

Brandon I should think so, too. Gave him a dozen Hail Marys, did you?

Edwin Wrong Church. But something like that. Lyd's invited him to supper.

Brandon (*rolling his eyes*) Oh, Lord. I should never have told her about the Borgias. (*He grins*)

Lydia (*in mock indignation*) One more crack about my cooking skills and you'll be doing your own meals.

Brandon Only joking, my precious. You can poison me any day.

Lydia (*dryly*) I might take you up on that.

Edwin (*to Brandon*) So what's this information you're bursting with?

Brandon Ah, yes. Well might you ask. But I'm not saying a word till I've unpacked my bag and filled my face with one of Lydia's lovely doorstops. I've not had a bite since breakfast and I'm ravenous. (*To Lydia*) Meat or cheese. I'm not fussy.

Lydia (*primly*) If you want sandwiches, you're out of luck. I'm not going near that kitchen again till they've stopped for lunch and I can open the fridge without it filling with sawdust. You can have a Mars Bar if you're that desperate. Now sit and speak.

Brandon (*moving to the armchair* R) Well, just the outlines, then. I'll give you the full story later. (*He sits*)

Lydia sits on the settee arm R

Right. Well, before I went to Lincoln last Friday, I had a word or two with Helen Lilywhite.

Edwin (*nodding*) So Maurice Walker told us.

Brandon (*knowingly*) Yes. Well, more about him, later. (*Back to his narrative*) She was quite wary of me for the first few minutes, but once I'd assured her I was only exploring avenues and promised to let her see everything I wrote, she relaxed and gave me her blessing. The fly in the ointment was David Lilywhite. Wouldn't even talk about it, and left the place breathing fire. Anyway, the upshot was I got the full story from her and started digging into the background stuff once I got to Lincoln. It's where the boys came from originally. But you'd know that, I expect?

Lydia Not really. I mean—we never asked. As I told you in the letter, it was all over by the time we moved here, so we only knew what we'd heard around the village.

Brandon Well, to cut a long story short, they'd had a pretty normal childhood and both were altar boys at St Oswald's, which was where your Reverend Middlemarch was the incumbent. They even worked for the same firm till the accident happened. (*Grimacing*) Parents were killed in a rather nasty car smash when the boys were in their teens.

Lydia (*softly*) Oh, no.

Brandon According to a neighbour I managed to trace, Jason went completely off the rails. Drink. Drugs. Tattoos—he'd a rather rude specimen on his back that raised a few hackles when he showed it—and whenever there was trouble, he was usually involved. Most of David's salary went on bailing him out of various escapades, but finally he took off for the bright lights, leaving David to cope with the aftermath. Six weeks later, baby brother took an overdose and ended up in Lincoln General. Never went back to the house. It went on the market while he was in there and, when he came out, he vanished. Turned up later in Norwich and married an actress from the Maddermarket Theatre. Helen De Keyper. The present Mrs Lilywhite.

Edwin So—is any of this any use? For the book, I mean?

Brandon Oh, yes. If I decide to do it, I want as many details as possible.

Lydia So what happens now?

Brandon Well, I've already got Helen's story. How they met, etc. I've read through the cuttings on the actual murder and what the police got up to—the local library's helped with that—so the next step's to meet this Cranshawe woman and get her story so I can start fitting the pieces together and see if the idea's feasible. (*Hopefully*) I couldn't have that Mars Bar, could I? I really am starving.

Lydia (*pityingly*) I'd hate to see you expire from lack of nourishment. (*She rises*)

Brandon (*gratefully*) You're an angel.

Lydia (*moving to the door*) I know. I was saving it for myself.

Lydia exits

Edwin (*hesitantly*) It's nothing to do with me, Bran, but why do you need to see Mrs Cranshawe? I mean—she'd nothing to do with the murder, and what she said about the Lilywhites—well—we all know it wasn't true.

Brandon Then why tell the police a pack of lies?

Edwin I told you. She was upset about losing the tea-room.

Brandon (*shaking his head*) If I'd been in her place, and saw what she claimed she saw, the last ones I'd go running to would be the police.

Edwin (*blankly*) I'm sorry?

Brandon I'll explain later. But take it from me, the helpful Mrs Cranshawe's either not the brightest bulb in the lighting department, or she's more to do with Jason's murder than anyone's yet realized.

Edwin (*baffled*) Well—you'll be able to make your mind up shortly. She telephoned a while ago. She's coming round here to see you.

Brandon (*perking up*) Is she now? (*Frowning*) Why can't I go to her place?

Lydia enters with a Mars Bar

Edwin No idea.

Lydia (*displaying it*) One horribly fattening, calorie-loaded, Mars Bar. (*Tossing it to him*)

Brandon (*catching it*) Lifesaver. I love you forever.

Lydia Well, before you start stuffing your face, you can tell us what you found out about Maurice Walker. (*Moving to the* R *edge of the settee*)

Brandon (*remembering*) Oh, yes. I did mention him, didn't I? Well, it's nothing to do with this business, but he's not the cold-hearted monster he pretends he is. According to the village gossips, he's got a rather heavy crush on the delectable Helen Lilywhite.

Lydia (*surprised*) You're joking.

Brandon Which could explain his fire and brimstone act the day I arrived here.

Lydia (*perching on the settee arm*) Who did you get that from?

Brandon (*primly*) A writer never reveals his sources. (*Grinning*) But I heard the lady in the Spar shop discussing it with one of her customers.

Edwin (*exasperated*) Honestly. This village.

Lydia (*firmly*) It's disgraceful the way they tittle-tattle about everybody and everything. No sense of propriety or discretion at all. (*Eagerly*) What else did you hear?

Edwin (*shocked*) Lydia. Really.

Brandon (*lightly*) Only that we've been having a torrid affair since the day I got here. And Edwin's dipping into the Church funds.

Edwin and Lydia look stunned

Lydia They never.
Brandon (*grinning*) Of course they never, dummy. But you should have seen your face. (*Displaying the Mars Bar*) Now can I eat my Mars Bar?
Lydia (*snatching it off him, indignantly*) No, you can't. I'm eating it myself.

The door chimes sound

Edwin (*rising*) I'll go. (*Moving L, behind the settee and heading for the door*)
Lydia (*airily*) Tell them we're about to have lunch. (*Displaying the Mars Bar*)

Edwin shakes his head and exits

Brandon I really could do with something to eat, Lyddy.
Lydia Tough. (*Moving L, behind the settee*)
Brandon (*hopefully*) Half a Mars Bar?
Lydia Not even a morsel. (*Moving to armchair L*)
Brandon (*rising*) In that case, I'll unpack my bag and scoff the biscuits I took from the B and B. (*He picks up his bag*)
Lydia (*turning to him*) You didn't.
Brandon I certainly did. Compliments of the management.

Edwin enters followed by Gwendolyn Cranshawe. She is in her late sixties, thin-lipped, with a disapproving manner, but expensively dressed

Edwin (*as he enters*) Mrs Cranshawe.
Gwendolyn (*to Lydia; stiffly*) Lydia. (*She turns her head to regard Brandon*)
Brandon (*putting his bag down*) Brandon Walsh. (*He holds out his hand*)

Gwendolyn ignores it and he lowers it again

You wanted to see me, I believe?
Gwendolyn (*to Edwin*) May I be seated?
Edwin (*hastily*) Of course. Please do. (*He indicates the settee*)

Gwendolyn moves L *behind the settee and round to settle herself. Edwin moves* R *to behind the armchair*

Brandon So?

Gwendolyn I'm told you are here to write a book, Mr Walsh? About the tea-room murder?

Brandon I'm thinking about it. Yes.

Lydia perches on the armchair arm

Gwendolyn To what purpose, might I ask?

Brandon (*frowning*) I'm sorry?

Gwendolyn (*impatiently*) Do you write for remuneration? Or simply in the interest of truth?

Brandon (*lightly*) I try to combine the two, Mrs Cranshawe. The labourer's still worthy of his hire, I believe.

Gwendolyn (*coldly*) That all depends on the quality of his work, Mr Walsh.

Brandon (*pleasantly*) So... What can I do for you?

Gwendolyn I want a firm assurance that the evidence I gave to the police concerning this sordid crime will be given the same importance as any other person's. I do not want it swept under the carpet for its refusal to fit preconceived theories.

Brandon (*nodding*) I think I can grant you that, Mrs Cranshawe— providing the information is genuine.

Gwendolyn (*sharply*) Despite what you may have been told, Mr Walsh, I am not in the habit of bearing false witness. I saw and heard exactly what I said at the time.

Brandon Yet the police saw fit to ignore your statement.

Gwendolyn (*tightly*) Their investigation was a complete shambles. David Lilywhite should have been jailed without the slightest hesitation.

Brandon So you still think he killed his brother?

Gwendolyn (*flatly*) I do.

Brandon Despite his wife's assertion of his innocence?

Gwendolyn Wives have been known to conceal their husband's crimes, Mr Walsh.

Brandon And what about the other witness? Henry Wilson? He actually saw the killer leaving.

Gwendolyn (*firmly*) Henry Wilson saw no one. His statement was an obvious invention, designed to bolster his self-importance in the community, and should be completely ignored.

Lydia (*blurting out*) Because you prefer to think David killed his brother?

Gwendolyn (*to her; tartly*) Did Cain not kill his?

Brandon (*lightly*) But Cain had a motive, didn't he? He was jealous of his brother. The Lilywhites, from what I've gathered, had a very close relationship—though not as close as you suggested in your statement. So tell me—what would be David's motive?

Gwendolyn (*coolly*) I have no idea. The detection of crime has no interest for me. But I know he killed Jason Lilywhite as surely as I know my own name.

There is a short silence

Brandon Right. (*Moving L, behind the settee*) Well, I've read all the press reports, etc., and heard various stories, but what I'd really like to know—in your own words—is exactly what you told the police.

Gwendolyn (*after a slight pause*) It was the day after they arrived here. I have a keen interest in local flora, and was in the old quarry with my sketchbook—looking for inspiration—when I heard voices. At first I ignored them, but later, they became raised and angry and I suddenly realized the interlopers were heading in my direction. Naturally I was concerned. A lone woman in an abandoned quarry with violent men in close proximity, so I hid myself behind a pile of fallen rocks. A few moments later, they came into view.

Lydia And you recognized them?

Gwendolyn (*coldly*) Of course. I'd met them earlier. As they moved into the flat above the tea-room. Rather vulgar and not at all the type of people Athelston welcomes. (*To Brandon*) As I was saying, they were still arguing...waving their arms...shouting...and pulling at each other's clothing.

Brandon (*cutting in*) Could you hear what they were saying?

Gwendolyn Only partially. The sound was distorted by echoes, and the wind was in the trees. But I did hear one of them shout that he wasn't going to do it, and the other one replied saying, "In that case, I'll do it myself".

Edwin (*puzzled*) Do what?

Gwendolyn (*frostily*) I've no idea. But whatever it was, it was obviously the cause of their quarrel.

Brandon (*moving R again*) So what happened, then?

Gwendolyn They began to struggle. Several times they fell to the ground, then one of them burst into tears and the other man—(*distastefully*) embraced him.

Lydia Embraced?

Gwendolyn (*sharply*) Hugged him. Like a woman. I was so shocked, I had to turn away. I felt ill.

Brandon And then what happened?

Gwendolyn The next time I looked, one of them was—disrobing.

Brandon You're quite sure about that?

Gwendolyn (*acidly*) I may have been convent educated, Mr Walsh, but I'm also a widow and well aware what the naked male body looks like.

Brandon So you witnessed them having sex?

Gwendolyn (*snapping*) Certainly not. The moment I realised what was going to happen, I left the vicinity as quickly as possible .

Brandon And what did you do next?

Gwendolyn To say I was shocked would be an understatement. The idea of perverts running the village tea-room was utterly unthinkable. Which is when I pulled myself together and decided I had no choice but to speak to Reverend Middlemarch.

Edwin (*curious*) And what did he say?

Gwendolyn (*scowling*) Unfortunately, he'd left for a conference that very morning and didn't arrive back until the day after the murder. Naturally I approached the police when the news broke, but after initial interest, my information was totally ignored and I became the object of scurrilous gossip and petty-minded vandalism. And all for simply telling the truth.

Brandon But there were certain aspects of your story that proved erroneous, Mrs Cranshawe. David and Jason were brothers, not lovers, and the post-mortem on Jason revealed no trace of homosexual activity – a fact that was also confirmed by Reverend Middlemarch, who'd known them both from way back.

Gwendolyn (*stubbornly*) I saw what I saw.

Brandon (*flatly*) I wonder.

They all look at Brandon in surprise

Does the name Christopher Carter have any significance for you, Mrs Cranshawe?

Gwendolyn (*warily*) Why should it?

Brandon (*easily*) He ran a small health club in Norwich.

Gwendolyn So?

Brandon Correct me if I'm wrong, but according to my information, most of the money tied up in the business appeared to be yours.

Gwendolyn (*balefully*) It was all a mistake. The man was a crook. A pervert. He deserved to be pilloried.

Brandon (*pressing*) But you were in business together?

Gwendolyn (*icily*) My dealings with Mr Carter are none of your concern.

Brandon (*lightly*) Perhaps not. But they did concern the police when they had to arrest him, didn't they?

Edwin and Lydia gape at him

Gwendolyn (*rising*) I refuse to listen to this…nonsense. I came here in all good faith to assist with your investigation and will not be subjected to malicious innuendo and false accusations. (*To Edwin and Lydia*) My apologies for intruding. (*Heading for the door, then turning back*) And if one word concerning that incident appears in your contemptible book, I shall take great pleasure in suing you for every penny you have.

She exits

Lydia (*standing*) What was all that about?

Brandon (*releasing a deep breath*) Just another ingredient for the cake mix. After reading all the other stuff, I couldn't help wondering why she'd tried to pin a gay label on the Lilywhites, so I did a bit more digging into her past. (*Dryly*) It's amazing what you can dredge up from the Internet.

Edwin (*moving down to him*) And what did you find?

Brandon About fifteen years ago, the lovely Widow Cranshawe teamed up with Christopher Carter, to run a rather exclusive health club. She coughed up most of the cash, and left him to run the place as though it were his own. For a few years it was all sweetness and light, then she decided she needed her money back to buy a place in Spain. Carter wasn't impressed and refused to sell his share, leaving her with her nose out of joint. Then suddenly the rumours started. Not only was Carter toning bodies, he was renting some of them out for immoral purposes.

Lydia (*shocked*) No.

Brandon The police received a tip-off and raided the place with the media in full pursuit. A teenage tearaway claimed Carter had been abusing him since the club opened, and within weeks, everything fell apart. Carter went to jail, the club closed, and Widow Cranshawe took her money and ran. Three months later, the kid confessed she'd paid him to commit perjury. (*He sits on the settee arm*)

Edwin (*indignantly*) Surely she didn't get away with it?

Brandon (*nodding*) By the time they picked her up for questioning, their one and only witness had vanished, and the case was dismissed. They knew, of course. They just couldn't prove it without him.

Edwin So that's what you meant when you said that if you were in her shoes, you wouldn't have gone near the police?

Brandon Exactly. But there's something else at the back of my mind. And if I'm right, it could put a whole different slant on things.
Lydia What is it?
Brandon Guess where they found her?

Edwin and Lydia look blank

At the British Embassy in Spain, complaining she'd been swindled out of a large sum of cash in a Valencian land scam. Now I could be wrong, but I've a strong suspicion that the man responsible was our old friend Jason Lilywhite. And if it was, it explains why she came up with the story she told the police. It was a straightforward case of revenge and character assassination.
Edwin (*puzzled*) But what would be the point? If Jason was the man who swindled her, he'd already been punished? Why involve David?
Lydia (*helpfully*) Could be frustration. She couldn't hurt Jason for what he'd done, so she took it out on his brother.
Edwin (*unhappily*) I suppose so. But even if you're right, I don't see how it helps anyone find out who the murderer was.
Brandon (*thoughtfully*) It might. If I could prove the man who swindled her was Jason Lilywhite. (*Explaining*) We already know she paid someone to accuse her ex-business partner. How do we know she didn't hire the man who killed Jason?
Lydia (*doubtfully*) She'd have had to move fast. They were only in the village a couple of days before it happened. Where would she find a murderer? She could hardly look one up in the Yellow Pages.
Brandon (*grinning*) You're right. I'm clutching at straws. Once I get my detective hat on, I come up with all kinds of theories. Mainly idiotic, I confess, but I do get better as the clues fall into place.
Edwin (*remembering*) And speaking of clues... According to Mrs Pashley, there may have been a second witness to the shooting. Roy Steadman, our gardener. But he didn't inform the police.
Lydia (*incredulously*) What?
Edwin (*wryly*) He fell foul of them a few years ago, and feels resentful about it.
Brandon Then he could be holding vital information. How do I contact him?
Lydia He'll be here tomorrow. (*Pleased*) Oh, Bran—we were right to ask you down here, weren't we? It was worth your coming?
Brandon (*nodding*) I wasn't too sure at first, but yes. The more I delve into this thing, the more interesting it gets. You may have a guest on your hands for the next few weeks.
Edwin So you've made up your mind, then? You are going to do a book?

Brandon (*grinning*) You can bet your life I am. If you want to stop me now, you'll have to kill me.

They all laugh happily as the Lights fade

ACT II

SCENE 1

A few hours later. The room is almost unchanged, but the crockery has been cleared away, as has Brandon's overnight bag. The french windows are closed. Daylight is fading and the lights are off, though the curtains are still open. The room is empty but the door is ajar and light seeps in from the hall

Laughter is heard, the door opens and Lydia enters, turning on the lights as she does so. She is followed by a grinning Brandon and Edwin

Lydia (*as she enters; primly*) Well, if you ask me, it's just another old wives' tale. (*She moves to the windows and closes the drapes*)

Brandon (*indignantly*) It's as true as I'm riding this bicycle. (*Moving to the armchair L*) Took five days to get it down again. (*He laughs and sits*)

Edwin (*moving to the settee*) And the look on his face when he found the pole covered in non-drying paint. If he'd known who was responsible, we'd all have been expelled.

The two men laugh hysterically

Lydia (*eyeing them in mock disapproval*) Small things amuse small minds. I suppose you want coffee now?

Edwin (*sobering*) Yes, please, darling.

Lydia I've a good mind to let you make it yourselves. Not a word of thanks for the lovely dinner I served up.

Brandon (*hastily*) It was divine, darling. The best Irish stew I've ever eaten.

Lydia (*glowering*) Chicken casserole, if you don't mind.

Brandon (*frowning*) Then what were all the bits of shamrock floating about in it?

Lydia Those were rosemary sprigs, heathen. To liven up the flavour.

Edwin Well, it certainly did that. Old greedy guts there had two helpings.

Brandon (*haughtily*) Only out of politeness.

Edwin Anyway, it's Ida we should be thanking. I'd no idea she was a culinary genius. Perhaps we should ask her to take over the catering as well as the cleaning?

Lydia (*indignantly*) After paying out a fortune for the new kitchen? In your dreams, sweetie-pie. I'll do my own cooking, thank you. I'll make that coffee.

She exits

Brandon (*sympathetically*) It was worth a try Eddie. (*Thoughtfully*) Rosemary sprigs, eh? I wondered what the odd taste was. Very moreish, though.

Edwin So we noticed. (*Standing*) Fancy a brandy? We've got the odd bottle or two. Thanks to grateful parishioners.

Brandon I wouldn't say no. It'll round off the meal nicely.

Edwin moves to the drinks cabinet. He takes out a bottle and two liqueur glasses and carries them to the table behind the settee

So…What about this Steadman character? Would he really keep quiet about being a witness?

Edwin (*pouring a drink*) We don't know that he was. It's just Sheila Pashley's opinion. But if what she said's true... Damn. It's empty. (*Examining the bottle then putting it down*) Never mind. There's a bottle of Polish Plum, somewhere. You want this—(*indicating the glass*) or that?

Brandon (*easily*) Whatever.

Edwin Better be this, then. I don't know how long the other one's been open. Does brandy go off? I haven't a clue. (*He hands Brandon the glass then moves to the cabinet again and begins rummaging*) He's a bit of an odd one, of course. Only been with us a few months, and not a regular worshipper. I think the last time we saw him there was at his mother's funeral. (*Pulling out a bottle*) Ah. Here we are. (*Moving back to the table unscrewing the cap*) Not too sociable, from all accounts, and known to be pretty sharp tempered. (*Hastily*) Not that we've had any problem with him. Quite the opposite. But in view of his past history, I suppose he might be inclined to keep his mouth shut. (*Pouring a drink*) Though I'm sure he'd have said something if David had been arrested.

Brandon And speaking of David, I'm still puzzled by his reaction to my doing a book. I mean, you'd think he'd want to help find his brother's killer, wouldn't you? (*He sips at his drink*)

The door chimes sound

Edwin I'm sure he does. (*He re-caps the bottle*) But they went through a pretty bad time, as I told you. The idea of raking it all up again mightn't appeal too much. (*He picks up his drink and moves round to sit on the settee again*) It's one of the reasons I wasn't too sure myself about getting you involved. But you know what Lydia's like. Can't bear a mystery. And as the police don't seem to have done anything about it for the past few years, she thought you might find it interesting. (*He drinks*)

The door chimes sound again

Brandon Want me to get that?
Edwin (*shaking his head*) Lyd'll do it. Probably Mrs Norton with the new altar cloth. She said she'd bring it round tonight.

The door chimes sound again

(*Rolling his eyes*) Better check. (*He puts his glass down*) Back in a minute.

He rises and exits

(*Off; surprised*) Helen?
Helen (*off*) Sorry to bother you, but——
Edwin (*off*) Not at all. Not at all. Come in.

Helen enters, followed by Edwin. She is dressed for an evening out

Brandon rises

What can I do for you?
Helen (*turning to Edwin anxiously*) You've not seen David, have you? I can't find him anywhere.
Edwin (*at a loss*) Well...not since yesterday. Outside the *Plough*, I think. (*Frowning*) Is something wrong?
Helen (*helplessly*) I don't know. I mean—he went out after we closed up and hasn't come back yet. It's almost three hours.
Brandon (*frowning*) Did he say where he was going?
Helen (*distractedly*) Just to meet someone and post a few letters. (*Worried*) I can't think what's happened to him.
Edwin (*lightly*) Not a great deal, I'm sure. He's most likely lost track of time. (*Smiling*) I'm always doing it.

Helen (*protesting*) But we're going out for dinner. He knows that.

Edwin (*reassuringly*) Then he's bound to be back.

Lydia enters behind them, looking rather unsteady

Lydia (*wanly*) Sorry I couldn't get the door. Bit of an emergency. (*Forcing a smile*) 'Lo, Helen.

Helen (*concerned*) Are you all right? You look awful.

Lydia (*lightly*) Too much cream in the casserole, I expect.

Brandon It was fine for me. But I could eat cream by the bucketful. (*Frowning*) Hadn't you better sit down? I'll see to the coffees.

Lydia (*moving to the armchair* R) It's all in hand. No need to panic. But I will sit down for the minute. (*Subsiding into the chair*)

Edwin (*moving to the windows*) I'll open the windows, shall I? It's getting a little warm in here.

Brandon (*rubbing his temple*) Mmm. It is a bit on the stuffy side. A breath of night air could do us all good. (*He sips at his drink*)

Edwin opens the curtains, fumbles with the knobs and opens the french windows

Edwin (*drawing a deep breath*) That's better. (*He moves to stand behind Lydia's chair*)

Lydia (*to Helen; with forced brightness*) So what brings you here tonight?

Edwin (*squeezing Lydia's shoulders gently*) She seems to have lost David.

Helen (*apologetically*) I was hoping he might be here. We had a talk last night. (*Glancing at Brandon*) About Mr Walsh. And he agreed to speak to him. (*To Brandon*) You've got to understand how upset he was. I know it's been four years, but they were very close. He loved Jason. Absolutely worshipped him.

Brandon (*murmuring*) Of course.

Helen (*embarrassed*) I never really liked him myself. Don't ask me why because I couldn't tell you. There was just something about him that really irked me. (*Hastily*) Though David doesn't know, of course. When he came out of prison, I was a bit put out that he moved down here with us. But as it turned out, he saved our lives. If it hadn't been for him, we'd both be dead.

Edwin (*quietly*) The Lord certainly moves in mysterious ways.

Lydia And how did he get in? The murderer, I mean?

Helen (*shaking her head*) We've no idea. He was just there. Gun pointing straight at us. It was like something from a nightmare.

Lydia (*curious*) Did he say anything?

Helen I've no idea. I was so terrified, I couldn't even think.

Edwin No chance of recognising him?

Helen (*shaking her head*) It was dark and he was wearing a mask. All I could see were his eyes. David shouted at him—asking what he was doing there—but he just kept pointing the gun at us. Then, suddenly, the stair light came on as Jason arrived home, and he panicked. Before we could move, he ran out of the bedroom, on to the landing and fired both barrels. David went after him, but it was too late. He'd gone down the stairs and vanished.

Brandon (*to Edwin*) She told me all this on Friday. No point in repeating it now. I'll fill you in later.

Helen (*almost dreamily*) That's when he started screaming—David, I mean—and I knew something terrible had happened. I got out of bed, went on to the landing and looked down. He was sitting on the floor holding Jason's body and both of them were covered in blood. (*She relives the moment, then speaks more matter-of-factly*) I tried to call the police, of course—and an ambulance—but the line was dead. He'd cut the wires before coming upstairs.

Lydia Thank goodness Henry was going by.

Helen (*nodding*) But it was nearly half an hour before anyone arrived. (*Wryly*) Apparently Saturday's a bad night. We both were in shock. And it was too late for Jason. He must have died instantly. (*Quietly*) I can't remember anything about the next few hours. The doctor sedated me, but they couldn't separate the boys. The ambulance had to take them both.

Edwin Such a pointless tragedy.

Helen We hardly knew anyone, of course. Neither of us had family, and being new to the area there were no friends——

Edwin (*interrupting*) Except Reverend Middlemarch.

Lydia Who happened to be away, if you remember?

Helen So a policewoman stayed with me till David came home again. I'll never forget his face till the day I die. He must have aged ten years. (*Bitterly*) And on top of it all, that evil bitch Cranshawe went running to the police with her pack of lies and they turned up at the flat to accuse him of killing Jason. (*In disbelief*) Can you believe it? David... of all people. The kindest, most gentle man who ever lived, killing his own brother. (*Pulling herself together*) I saw her crossing the street that afternoon and that's what triggered me off again. I'd worked with some bastards in the theatre, but she was another thing altogether. If Maurice Walker hadn't pulled me off her, I'd have strangled her in the middle of Castle Street with a dozen or so witnesses watching me.

Brandon No wonder you had a breakdown. (*He perches on the armchair arm* L)

Helen Oh. So you know about that do you? (*Wryly*) Yes. Well...It's part of the reason, I suppose. But what tipped me over the edge was Reverend Middlemarch dying.

Edwin (*surprised*) Jack?

Helen I came here to see him the night after David came back from the hospital. I'd heard so much about him, and he'd defended them to the police, so I wanted to thank him personally, tell him David was back, and invite him to dinner when things had settled down. The lights were on, but he wasn't in, so I went down to the Twelve Apostles to see if he was there.

Edwin suddenly winces and clutches at his stomach. No one notices

Lydia (*realising*) Don't say it was you who found him?

Helen (*nodding*) He'd been dead about twenty minutes. The next thing I knew I was in hospital. I never want to hear the word Valium again.

Edwin (*uneasily*) Excuse me a minute. (*Edging towards the open window*)

Lydia (*looking at him*) What is it?

Edwin (*forcing a smile*) Think I saw someone in the garden. I'll just make sure.

Edwin hurriedly exits, clutching his stomach

Brandon (*rising*) Eddie? (*Putting his glass on the table behind the settee*)

Lydia (*rising and hurrying to the window to look out*) Edwin? (*Stepping back hastily*) Oh. He's being sick. (*Realizing*) It must be the casserole.

Brandon Can't be. I had twice as much as anybody, and I'm all right. More likely the plum brandy. He said it was pretty old.

Lydia I'd better go to him.

She exits into the garden

Brandon (*to Helen*) Sorry about that. He always did have a sensitive stomach. Couldn't face liver and onions, or devilled kidneys... even at school. And as for tapioca pudding... the less said the better. (*He grins*)

Helen (*uneasily*) Hadn't you better call a doctor?

Brandon (*airily*) No need for that. A mug of black coffee'll do him the world of good. Once he's got it off his—er—chest, he'll be right as rain.

The door chimes sound, urgently, and Brandon glances into the garden

I'll just see who that is.

He exits into the hall

Maurice (*off, loudly*) Is Helen here?
Brandon (*off, startled*) Hoy.

Maurice bursts into the room and sees Helen. He is in his chef's whites

Maurice (*breathlessly*) Thank God. You'd better come. Quick.
Helen What?
Maurice (*grabbing Helen's arm*) It's David.

Brandon enters behind them

Helen (*alarmed*) What about him?
Maurice He's been hurt. In the Prentice quarry.
Helen (*uncomprehending*) What?
Maurice One of the lads found him. Walking his dogs. Looks like someone's attacked him. There's blood all over his head.
Helen (*anguished*) Oh, my God.

She pulls herself free and hurries out of the room

Maurice turns to follow, but Brandon grabs his arm

Brandon (*to Maurice*) How is he?
Maurice How should I know? (*Shaking himself free*) I've been in the kitchen all night. They've been knocking every door in the village for the past fifteen minutes. If Amy Ferris hadn't spotted her passing Thorne Cottage, I'd never have thought of looking for her here.
Brandon Why not?
Maurice (*dryly*) They'd an eight-thirty booking at my place. And she'd hardly be tucking into one of Ida Cornish's gastronomical delights before sitting down to a bit of real cooking, now would she?
Brandon Having never had the pleasure, I couldn't say, but I'll take your word for it. (*Curiously*) So what was he doing in this quarry you mentioned? I presume it's the same one as before?
Maurice (*tightly*) You'll have to ask him yourself. Providing he's alive. I know nothing except what I've told you. Now if you don't mind, the *Plough*'s full of customers and I'm supposed to be cooking.

He exits

Brandon (*looking after him*) Exit pursued by a bear.

Lydia hurriedly enters through the french windows and he turns to her

How is he?

Lydia (*moving towards the door*) He wants a drink. There's some tonic water in the fridge. (*Noticing Helen has gone*) Where's Helen?

Brandon (*quickly*) Just gone. There's been bad news. David's been attacked.

Lydia (*stopping in her tracks*) What?

Brandon In the Prentice quarry.

Lydia (*stricken*) Oh, my God. (*Hastily*) How is he? Not dead?

Brandon Not that I know. A chap and his dogs found him.

Lydia (*horrified*) What was he doing in the quarry? David, I mean.

Brandon Haven't a clue. Unless he was meeting somebody.

Lydia In the quarry? At this time of night?

Brandon Depends when it happened. It could have been earlier. She said he went out to meet someone. (*He brushes his neck, absently*)

Lydia Look after Edwin. I'd better see if I can help.

Brandon What can you do? You're no nurse.

Lydia (*snapping*) For her, stupid. Not him. (*She gives a sudden gasp of pain and clutches at her stomach*)

Brandon (*concerned*) Lyd? (*He hurries to her*)

Lydia (*panting*) I'm all right. It's nothing. Just do as I... (*She gives another gasp and collapses into his arms*)

Brandon (*startled*) Lydia. (*He moves her to the settee and lowers her on to it; anxiously*) Lydia? (*He hurries to the windows and calls*) Eddie. Come quick. It's Lydia.

After a moment, Edwin appears looking very unsteady and ill. He is wiping at his mouth

She's collapsed. (*Indicating Lydia*)

Edwin (*staggering forward*) Call a doctor. Tell him... (*He sways and falls to his knees*) Food poison... (*He collapses on to the floor and lies still*)

Brandon gazes at him in disbelief, then hurries to the phone and begins to dial. As he does so, the door chimes sound

Brandon (*shouting*) Help. Help. (*Into the phone*) Come on, come on. (*Beat*) Thank God. We need an ambulance. Quickly. There's been a poisoning. (*Beat*) Athelstone vicarage. The vicar and his wife. They're both unconscious.

The door opens and Ida appears. She is wearing an outdoor coat and is carrying a covered dish and a set of house keys

Ida   (*as she enters*) I thought you might like a dessert, so I—(*She sees Edwin and stops in shock*) Oh. (*Dropping the dish and keys*)

Brandon   (*into the phone*) What's it matter who I am? Just send somebody quick. (*He puts the phone down and turns to Ida*) What the hell did you put in that casserole? (*He hurries to Edwin and kneels beside him*)

Ida   (*stunned*) Casserole? (*She looks down at the dropped dish*)

Brandon   (*angrily*) The one you brought over tonight? What was in it?

Ida   (*flustered*) Just the usual. Chicken, onions, stock and a bit of cornflour. (*She notices Lydia for the first time and gasps*)

Brandon   (*attempting to revive Edwin*) And what else?

Ida   A few cashew nuts. (*Hastily*) Our Michael loved cashews in his casseroles. (*Anxiously*) They're not allergic to them, are they?

Brandon   (*ignoring this*) What else?

Ida   (*helplessly*) Nothing. Well... seasoning, of course. Salt... Pepper...

Brandon   Rosemary.

Ida   (*looking blank*) Rosemary? (*Baffled*) No.

Brandon   (*snapping*) What do you mean, no?

Ida   (*reasonably*) They don't all like the taste, do they?

Brandon   (*turning to her*) But there were handfuls of it in that casserole.

Ida   (*firmly*) Not when it left my house, there wasn't. I've never used rosemary since the day my husband died.

Brandon   Then how did it get into the casserole?

Ida   (*indignantly*) You're not saying my casserole's something to do with this? I was making casseroles before you were born. And besides, I had some of it for my own dinner, and there's nothing wrong with me.

Brandon   (*rising*) No, no. I'm not blaming you.

Ida   (*huffily*) I should hope not.

Brandon   I'm just trying to find out what's happened. (*He glances across at Lydia and realises*) Oh, no. She must have added it.

Ida   What?

Brandon   She's the world's worst cook and we were always pulling her leg about it. She was probably trying to impress us by improving on what you'd made. I'd better check the kitchen. (*Moving towards the door*)

Ida   (*firmly*) I can do that. You'd best stay here with them. (*Glancing at*

Lydia) She looks awful.
Brandon Right.

Ida scoops up the dropped dish and exits

(*Shaking his head*) God, it's so hot in here. (*He moves unsteadily to Lydia and feels her forehead; softly*) What was it, Lyd? What the hell did you use? (*He straightens, then sways dizzily and clutches at the settee back to steady himself. He looks at his hand on the settee, then lurches back in panic*) Ahhhhh. (*Staring at the settee back*) Don't move, Lyd. If you can hear me, for God's sake don't move. There's something inside the settee. I can see it moving (*Stunned*) A snake. It's a snake. A bloody big rattlesnake. (*Looking frantically around for a weapon*) Don't worry. I can kill it. I won't let it hurt you. (*He suddenly gives a loud gasp and doubles with pain*) Oh, my God. It's bitten me. It's bitten me. (*Frantically*) Get it off me. Get it off. (*Twisting around frantically and yelling*) Mrs Cornish. Ida. Don't come in. Don't come in. (*He gives another loud gasp then collapses on to the floor*)

There is a moment's pause, then Ida hurries in looking flustered

Ida (*concerned*) What's happened? What is it?

She sees Brandon, then lets out a horrified scream. She continues to scream as the Lights rapidly fade to Black-out

SCENE 2

Six weeks later. Wednesday morning. Little has changed. Drinks and bottle have been cleared, the room is reasonably tidy and fresh flowers are in the vase. The french windows are open and the sound of a lawnmower can be heard

After a moment, Sheila enters carrying a tray holding tea things and a plate of sliced cake. She deposits these on the coffee table, then moves to the french windows

Sheila (*calling*) Roy? Roy? Tea's up.

She returns to the settee, sits and begins pouring tea into the mugs. As she does so, the sound of the mower dies

A moment later, Roy enters through the french window. His perspiration-soaked shirt is unbuttoned to the waist exposing a grimy vest

Roy (*moving to* R *of the settee*) I'm ready for this, I can tell you. A real bugger, that bottom end is. All tree roots and bloody mole hills.

Sheila (*chiding*) Now, now. You are in the vicarage.

Roy (*grunting*) It's heard worse than anything I've said here.

Sheila (*primly*) Yes. Well, we needn't go into that. (*Smiling graciously*) Sit yourself down and have your tea. (*She extends a mug to him*)

Roy (*taking it*) Are you sure it won't upset her ladyship?

Sheila She's gone to London to see her daughters. I'm in charge till she's back again.

Roy And when'll that be? (*He sits in the armchair* R)

Sheila Thursday night, so I'm told. Would you like a slice of fruit cake? (*Picking up the plate*) It's homemade.

Roy Not for me, thanks. (*Sipping at the tea noisily*) How's Vicar doing?

Sheila (*hesitantly*) Hard to say, really. He's not said much since he came out of hospital. (*Lowering her voice*) To tell you the truth, I'm surprised he's still here. At the vicarage, I mean. Not like Lydia and Mr Walsh. I still can't believe they're dead. None of us can. (*She takes a slice of cake and puts the plate down*)

Roy (*heavily*) Well, you know what they say? In the midst of life...

Sheila Yes. But fancy poisoning yourself. Even if it was by accident. You'd have thought even she could tell the difference between rosemary sprigs and yew leaves. (*She nibbles at the slice of cake*)

Roy (*glancing at her*) Could you?

Sheila (*surprised*) Well, of course I could. I might not be much of a gardener, but I can tell a herb from a tree. (*Earnestly*) If Agatha Christie were still alive, she'd have Miss Marple on her way here, right this minute.

Roy (*frowning*) Who?

Sheila Miss Marple. Her detective woman. You must have seen her on television or read the books. Dotty as they come, but always manages to solve the murders.

Roy (*sourly*) I've more to do with my time than read books and watch television. But why'd we want a detective?

Sheila Because it'd make a good plot if she happened to be looking for one. (*Dramatically*) Vicar's wife and best friend murdered with a poisoned casserole...

Roy (*puzzled*) But they weren't murdered.

Sheila (*exasperated*) I know they weren't. But she could say they

were, couldn't she? No point in writing a murder if it's all accidental.
(*Continuing happily*) Another body in the quarry, and mysterious clues
all over the village. It could almost write itself (*She puts the uneaten
piece of cake down on to a side plate*)

Roy (*blankly*) What mysterious clues?

Sheila The ones in the song. (*Singing brightly*) "I'll sing you one, O...
Green grow the rushes, O... What is your one, O?... One is one and all
alone... And evermore shall be so..."

Roy stares at her

You must remember it. You sang it at school. Everybody did. (*Brightly*)
Well, it's all here. In the village. The Lilywhite boys. The Seven Stars,
The Twelve Apostles...everything.

Roy (*dryly*) I'd better get back to that mowing. (*He stands and indicates
his mug*) I'll leave this on the window ledge when I've finished.
(*Turning to exit through the french windows*)

Sheila You don't see it, do you? (*Pleased with herself*) It was Henry
Wilson who gave me the idea. Remember the break-in at the memorial
hall a few weeks back? Well, that's where the cymbals came from.
Stan Patterson's drum kit. Whoever took them left them tied to Henry's
back door for a joke. He told me about it himself. And when I thought
about it afterwards, I could see how it fitted. (*Wistfully*) It's a pity Mr
Walsh is dead. I could have suggested it to him.

Roy (*puzzled*) What?

Sheila The storyline, of course. (*Enthusing*) Jason and David Lilywhite,
could be the Two, O, O's, couldn't they? They've got the names, to
start with and they're both clothèd in green now they're buried in
Athelston cemetery. The rivals could be Lena and Patrick Jackson and
Doris Weatherby. They've been at loggerheads for as long as I can
remember...

Roy (*pointedly*) Yes. And there'd be no prize for naming the gospel
makers, either. Except they should be called the gossip-mongers.

Sheila (*nodding*) I couldn't agree with you more. (*Ticking them off on her
fingers*) Molly Fisher, Gladys Appleton, Amy Ferris. (*Disapprovingly*)
They spread rumours round this place like flu. (*Primly*) I wouldn't have
the nerve myself. (*Continuing*) Then Five's the cymbals on Henry's
door. Six is the Walker family—I know there's only five of them if
you count the daughter-in-law, but they certainly fancy themselves—
and Seven's the *Plough*. (*Beaming*)

Roy (*baffled*) How do you work that out? There's nothing in the song
about a pub.

Sheila (*smirking*) No. But when I was at school, the plough was another

name for the Big Dipper. Because of its shape, you see? It's got seven
stars.

Roy And what about the rest of the song?

Sheila Well...we've got the Twelve Apostles church, haven't we?
But I'm sure Mr Walsh could have found something to fit the other
things...

Roy (*acidly*) He caused enough problems as it was, without turning it
into a trashy detective story. Perhaps folk'll get a bit of peace, now
he's out of the way.

Sheila (*slightly hurt*) I don't think that's very nice, Mr Steadman. I
wouldn't have minded having my name in his book. He did say he'd
acknowledge everybody that helped with his research, didn't he? And
you'd have had a mention, as well.

Roy (*surprised*) Me? Why should I be in his book?

Sheila Well—he'd have wanted to know what you saw the night Jason
Lilywhite got killed, wouldn't he?

Roy (*sharply*) Who says I saw anything?

Sheila (*easily*) Well... I know you didn't tell the police, but I saw you
go down Castle Street myself. I was sitting by the window in my
bedroom. You couldn't have missed whoever was running away.

Roy (*harshly*) Well, I bloody well did, didn't I? It was nearly midnight.
I saw nothing that night.

He moves closer to her, face grim and she shrinks back

And you say anything otherwise, you'll have me to answer to. All
right? (*More forcefully*) All right?

*Sheila's mouth opens with shock and she nods timidly. He turns and
moves to the french windows before turning again to glare at her*

Remember.

He exits, still holding the mug

*Sheila snatches up her tea and takes a hasty gulp at it. There is the sound
of door chimes which startles her*

She rises, composes herself, then bustles out

*A moment later, Gwendolyn enters. She is dressed like a fashion plate
for an exclusive magazine, and carries a small jar of honey. Sheila
follows her into the room, anxiously*

Gwendolyn (*icily*) I have an appointment with Reverend Summerfield.

Sheila (*fretting*) He's not here, I'm afraid. He had a meeting with Bishop Arthur and I'm not sure when he'll be back.

Gwendolyn (*firmly*) Eleven o'clock was our agreed time. I shall wait until then.

Sheila (*after a slight pause*) Can I get you a cup of tea?

Gwendolyn (*moving to the settee*) Do you have Earl Grey?

Sheila (*at a loss*) It's just what's in the caddy.

Gwendolyn Then, no. Thank you. (*She sits*)

Sheila (*uneasily*) Are you sure you don't mind? Being on your own. It's just that I'm upstairs, sorting Lydia's things out for charity.

Gwendolyn (*mildly surprised*) So soon?

Sheila He doesn't want them reminding him. It'd be six years next month, their anniversary. He just asked me to make sure they don't go to the shop in Hobbs Lane. Wouldn't be nice seeing somebody local in his wife's clothes, would it? (*Helplessly*) I don't know what's happening with Mr Walsh's things. He'd no family apparently, so they're still upstairs in the spare bedroom. Clothes, notebooks, everything he brought with him. I'd no idea he was so well known.

Gwendolyn (*dryly*) His obituary was in *The Times*.

Sheila (*slightly embarrassed*) I don't read anything but the local, but the man on television said he was highly regarded in his field and his research was impressive.

Gwendolyn (*coldly*) He could hardly have said otherwise. Notability in a non-fiction writer rarely results from erroneous research. (*Pointedly*) You said you were busy.

Sheila (*remembering*) Oh. Yes. I'd better get on with it, then.

Sheila hesitates, as though about to speak again, then smiles weakly and exits

Gwendolyn puts the jar of honey beside her and sits there, face devoid of emotion. After a moment she glances at her watch, then returns to immobility

A few more seconds pass, then Edwin enters the room. He appears to have aged and his whole demeanour is subdued

Edwin (*seeing Gwendolyn*) Ah.

Gwendolyn turns her head to him

You've arrived then? (*Moving down to R of her*) Sorry I couldn't be here. I had to have a word with the bishop. You've not been waiting long?

Gwendolyn A few moments. Nothing untowards.

Edwin Can I offer you some tea?

Gwendolyn (*primly*) No, thank you. I'd prefer to proceed with the matter to hand.

Edwin Yes. Of course. (*He sits in the armchair* R)

Gwendolyn (*gathering herself*) For the past few weeks, I've been in London. Which is why I've been unable to extend commiserations on the death of Mrs Summerfield.

Edwin (*quietly*) Thank you.

Gwendolyn I shall, of course, be in my usual pew on Sunday morning.

Edwin smiles tiredly and nods

My reason for being here today, however, is in connection with Mr Walsh. His effects, I understand, are still in your possession?

Edwin (*puzzled*) At the moment, yes. I'm waiting for his executors——

Gwendolyn (*cutting in*) Who are?

Edwin (*taken aback*) I've no idea. (*Intuitively*) But if this is anything to do with his book, there's nothing for you to worry about. He'd only just started, so apart from his notes—I mean—he hadn't even—well... There won't be any book.

Gwendolyn Precisely my point. But I'm sure you'll agree that there should be?

Edwin (*staring at her*) I'm sorry?

Gwendolyn (*seething with indignation*) Since the death of Jason Lilywhite four years ago, I have been vilified by complete strangers— not to mention the residents of our own village—for merely speaking the truth. With your assistance, I shall vindicate myself at last and regain my good name and character.

Edwin (*confused*) I don't understand.

Gwendolyn As you know, I have always maintained that David Lilywhite murdered his brother, Jason. His subsequent suicide proves without doubt that my suspicions were correct.

Edwin (*puzzled*) Suicide? It was an accident.

Gwendolyn (*matter-of-factly*) Only according to the police. My own interpretation of the facts indicates a very different conclusion.

Edwin (*rising; a little irritated*) What exactly is it you want, Mrs Cranshawe? (*He moves behind the settee, restlessly*)

Gwendolyn I have a friend in London who runs a small publishing firm in Golden Square. Without going into details, I can reveal she has expressed a keen interest in Mr Walsh's book on the murder of Jason Lilywhite.

Edwin (*moving* L) I've already told you. There isn't a book.

Gwendolyn But there could be, Reverend Summerfield. If the executors agree, whatever information Mr Walsh had gathered—plus any ideas and opinions he may have noted down—could be ghost written by a reputable author and presented to the public in Mr Walsh's name.

Edwin (*turning to her*) For what reason?

Gwendolyn (*sharply*) If for nothing else, to repudiate the slurs on my character. With new information now in my possession, I can prove that every word I spoke concerning this sordid affair was nothing but the gospel truth.

Edwin (*tiredly*) And what exactly is this new information, Mrs Cranshawe?

Gwendolyn I prefer to keep that to myself at the moment. But a glance at Mr Walsh's notes could quickly confirm my conclusions. So if you wouldn't mind letting me see them.

Edwin I'm afraid that's out of the question. Until I've spoken with his executors, everything must remain where it is.

Gwendolyn There'd be no need to remove them. I could read them here and now.

Edwin (*firmly*) I'm sorry.

Gwendolyn (*tightening her lips*) Then it appears we have nothing further to discuss. (*Remembering the honey, she picks it up and rises*) I do not, however, intend to let the matter drop. I shall broach the subject with the appropriate persons at a future date. Thank you for your time. (*She moves to the door*)

Edwin (*following*) I'm truly sorry, but you must see my position. I will try to contact whoever it is and get their consent. Just give me a little time.

Gwendolyn (*after a momentary reflection*) I'll enquire again on Sunday. After the service.

Edwin Oh. (*Hesitating*) I—er—won't be there. (*He sighs and turns away*) It's what my meeting with the bishop was about. I'm resigning the living. Taking time out. I can't face staying here after—well—after what happened. Too many reminders.

Gwendolyn (*after a moment*) I see. (*Coldly*) We'll be sad to see you go.

Edwin (*wanly*) I doubt it. I've always been second best to Jack Middlemarch. Perhaps my successor will have better luck? (*He smiles sadly*)

Gwendolyn (*flatly*) One makes one's own luck, Reverend Summerfield. However, I'm sure your faith will sustain you.

Gwendolyn exits, closing the door

Roy steps through the french windows

Roy (*scowling*) Patronizing cow. What she knows about faith could be written on a poppy seed. (*Remembering*) Sorry, Vicar. But she gets up my nose like bloody chicken manure.

Edwin (*sharply*) Were you eavesdropping?

Roy (*shaking his head*) Just saw you moving about and wondered if you were all right. You don't look it, if you'll pardon my saying so. I'm surprised you're still with us. Not many survive taxine poisoning. You were damned lucky.

Edwin (*sitting tiredly on the settee*) That's a matter of opinion.

Roy Luckier than some I could mention. The medics can't do much when a shotgun blast takes half your head off.

Edwin (*sharply*) That's a bit insensitive, wouldn't you say?

Roy (*shrugging*) I speak as I see it.

Edwin (*looking down*) If you don't mind, Roy, I'm not really up to this.

Roy (*nodding*) Lack of sleep, I expect. I've noticed the lights, most nights. Thought you'd had a break-in at first, place being empty since the accident. If it hadn't been for you-know-who, we'd never have known you were back.

Edwin (*tiredly*) Look. Would you mind just leaving me alone, Roy? I need to clear my head.

Roy It's not your head clearing, you want. It's a decent meal. There's no nourishment in hospital food, no matter what they tell you and you're obviously not eating the rubbish she's serving up. A good stew's what you need. There's a couple of rabbits on the draining board. Fresh last night. Don't let 'em go to waste. (*He turns to exit*)

Edwin (*protesting*) I couldn't possibly...

Roy (*pausing*) Never look a gift horse in the mouth, Vicar. Only cost me a couple of shots and nobody's any the wiser.

Roy exits through the french windows

Edwin closes his eyes and sighs heavily. A moment later he opens them again and focuses on the tea tray. For a few seconds he studies it, then rising, picks up the tray and moves towards the door

As he does so, it opens and Sheila enters

Sheila (*beaming*) That's all sorted, then. Everything's in bags for the shop and her jewellery's separate on top of the dresser. (*Embarrassed*) I didn't know if—well—you know? There was anything you'd like to keep. Breaks your heart seeing it all lying there. (*Noticing the tray*) I'll take that, shall I? (*Taking it from him*) You put your feet up and relax.

Won't take a minute to do your lunch. Some nice oxtail soup and fresh
bread from Hansons'll pick you up no end. (*She turns to exit*)
Edwin (*tiredly*) I shouldn't bother, Mrs P. I'm not all that hungry.
A few
minutes' sleep will probably do me more good.
Sheila (*kindly*) Well, you know best, I'm sure. I'll see you're not
disturbed if you decide. (*Remembering*) Oh, and the bag in Mr Walsh's
old room. It's only for the dustbin. I popped it in there so it didn't get
mixed up with the others. (*Slightly concerned*) You didn't trip on it,
did you?
Edwin (*blankly*) Sorry?
Sheila When you went in. (*Hastily*) I never gave it a thought. Just
popped it inside to bring down later and didn't remember till I heard
you moving round in there.
Edwin (*bemused*) You must have been dreaming. I haven't been upstairs
this morning.
Sheila (*puzzled*) I could have sworn I heard somebody.
Edwin (*smiling*) Floorboards settling, most probably. There's no one
else in the house and certainly nothing worth stealing.
Sheila (*caustically*) There's some in the village'd steal anything
if it wasn't nailed down. And one of them's not a mile away, this
minute——

The door chimes sound

I'll get that.

Sheila hands Edwin the tray and exits

Edwin looks at the tray as though he's never seen it before

Maurice (*off*) How's he doing?

Edwin closes his eyes and shakes his head

Sheila (*off*) You'd better come in.

Sheila appears in the doorway

(*To Edwin; confidentially*) It's Maurice Walker.

She takes the tray from him, stepping aside to let Maurice enter

I told him you were feeling tired. He won't stay long.

She beams at them both and exits

Edwin (*forcing a smile*) Maurice. (*He indicates the settee*)
Maurice (*shaking Edwin's hand*) I heard you were back. Should have
come by sooner, but I wasn't sure. (*Breaking off*) How're you feeling?
(*He moves down to the settee*)
Edwin It gets easier as time passes.
Maurice (*sitting*) Weybourne, wasn't it? The old retreat on the seafront?
Did they take good care of you?
Edwin Couldn't have been kinder. (*Sitting in the armchair* R) And
thanks for all you did. Especially the flowers. (*Wanly*) She'd have
liked them very much.
Maurice (*uncomfortable*) Least we could do. We all miss her. (*After
a slight pause*) It was a good turnout. Most of the village, in fact.
(*Wryly*) Pity you couldn't have been there.
Edwin (*looking away*) Yes.
Maurice He stayed on afterwards. The bishop. Even spoke to Helen.
They buried David a few days earlier. Next to his brother.
Edwin (*softly*) Such a terrible tragedy. It must have destroyed her. First
Jason— and then her husband. (*He sighs*) I should call in to see her,
but I've hardly left the house since I returned. I feel so—so empty.
Maurice (*staunchly*) There's nobody'll blame you for that. It's been no
bed of roses for you. But if you were thinking of dropping in on her,
you'd better do it soon. She's selling the tea-room and going back to
Norwich. To live with her sister, or something.
Edwin (*nodding slowly*) I'd a feeling she might. (*More firmly*) I'll be
leaving myself, shortly. Can't possibly stay after everything that's
happened.
Maurice (*surprised*) But I thought——
Edwin There's something wrong with this village. I've known it ever
since we came here. (*He rises and moves behind the settee*) Oh, I
know it's picturesque and, on the surface, the people are no worse and
no better than anywhere else I could mention. But all the same, there's
a sense of— evil about it. A kind of malevolence.
Maurice (*taken aback*) I can't say I've noticed.
Edwin (*protesting*) You mentioned it yourself. A few weeks ago. The
constant gossip. The sly remarks. Vicious innuendo. It's like Dante's
vision of hell.
Maurice (*helplessly*) It's life in a village. (*Frowning*) Has somebody
said something?
Edwin (*after a moment*) No. (*Pause*) No. It's just that I've had enough.
Without Lydia, there's nothing for me here. I've already spoken to the
bishop and I'll be gone by the end of the month. (*Moving down* L)
Maurice (*frowning*) Sorry to hear it. Have you anywhere in mind? I
mean—is your family——?

Edwin (*shaking his head*) Just a cousin. In New Zealand. But we've not been in contact for years. I think he's afraid of my disapproval.

Maurice looks puzzled

(*Explaining*) He lives with his boyfriend. Loath as I am to admit it, you're looking at the last of the Summerfields.

Maurice (*lightly*) Well…there's still time. You're only a youngster. Give it a few years and who knows?

Edwin (*shaking his head*) I've had the tests. There isn't a hope.

Maurice (*frowning*) But— you had a family? You mentioned it.

Edwin (*wanly*) I wasn't the father. (*Sitting on the chair arm*) I saw her at a party when we were teenagers and fell for her, hook, line, and sinker. The only trouble was, she was about to get engaged to some brilliant academic at Reading University. It was years before we ran into each other again but I'd never forgotten her. I was a curate in my first parish, and Bran was celebrating the publication of his latest book. Couldn't believe my eyes when I spotted her in the crowd. She'd long since broken off her engagement, and found it amusing I'd been holding a torch for her since schooldays. A few weeks later, she told me she was pregnant. The father had vanished and she wanted advice on what to do.

Maurice So—?

Edwin (*rising*) I asked her to marry me. Told her I didn't care who the father was. We'd bring it up as our own and no one would be any the wiser. (*Resignedly*) She lost the baby five weeks after the wedding. (*Forcing a smile and moving back* R) We tried for another, of course, but it never happened so, after three years, we took the tests. I was infertile and she was devastated. We wanted a family so much.

Maurice Did you never think of adopting?

Edwin (*shaking his head*) It was God's decision and we had to stand by it. But we still had each other. That was the important thing. As long as we had each other, we'd survive. But now… (*His voice tails off*)

There is a short silence

Maurice (*heavily*) Well… we'll be sad to lose you. Village won't be the same. (*Bewildered*) I still can't believe it happened. She was no Nigella Lawson, but mistaking yew sprigs for rosemary—it doesn't make sense.

Edwin (*turning to face Maurice; puzzled*) In what way?

Maurice She spent time in the *Plough*'s kitchen with me. Remember? Picking up tips and a few basic recipes. I took her through the herbs and spice range a dozen times. The smell alone, should have told her she was picking the wrong thing, never mind the actual plant. Like I said...it doesn't make sense. She had her culinary faults, but she was no idiot.

Edwin (*staring at him*) My God. (*He steadies himself on the armchair*)

Maurice (*puzzled*) What is it?

Edwin (*dazedly*) You've just confirmed what's been driving me mad. I was right. (*He sits heavily on the arm*)

Maurice (*blankly*) What about?

Edwin (*slowly*) I knew there was something that didn't add up. I just couldn't think what it was. (*More animated*) Of course she knew the difference between a yew tree and rosemary. She mentioned it to me the day she died. (*Trying to recall*) The one by the lychgate. It needed trimming, or something. (*Rising again*) Don't you see? It wasn't Lyd who did it. It wasn't her who poisoned us.

Maurice gapes at him

(*Moving L, behind the settee again*) It had nothing to do with us. It was Bran they wanted to stop. We were just in the wrong place at the wrong time. (*Realizing*) Oh, my God. (*Turning to stare at Maurice*) It was my fault. I'm the one who brought him here. If it hadn't been for me, they'd both be still alive.

Maurice (*baffled*) Hang on. Hang on. You've lost me.

Edwin (*distractedly*) There'd been vandalism in the churchyard. Nothing major, but a few of the stones were defaced and one of them happened to be Jason Lilywhite's. We got talking with Henry Wilson about the murder and I said if the police appeared to have written it off, maybe Bran would be interested in digging for clues. Lydia was all for it, dropped him a line, and the following week he was here.

Maurice (*a little sheepish*) I remember.

Edwin At first he wasn't too keen on the idea and we couldn't understand why everyone seemed so upset about it. We were only doing it for Helen and David. But the more digging he did, the keener he got. And no one dug deeper than Bran. He'd half-filled a notebook with things he'd found out, and some of them, even the police hadn't bothered to look for. It was only a matter of time before he'd know who'd killed Jason Lilywhite— and from what he hinted, it wasn't some mysterious foreigner. (*Heavily*) And that's why he had to be stopped.

Maurice (*incredulously*) You mean... by someone in Athelston? (*Pause*) But who?

Edwin I've no idea. But I'm going to find out. Whoever slipped that poison into Ida Cornish's casserole, killed Lydia, too—and they're not going to get away with it.

Maurice (*rising*) I'd not be too hasty, if I was you. You can't say for certain there was anybody else involved. It could have been Lydia's mistake. There was no one else in the house when it happened, was there?

Edwin The kitchen door was open to let the dust settle. We'd had the workmen in. Remember? Half the village knew. Anyone could have walked through.

Maurice And how'd they know you'd have a casserole in the oven?

Edwin (*bitterly*) In this village?

Maurice (*soothingly*) Be reasonable, Vicar, and think about it. If anybody had wanted to kill him, they'd not have intended harming Lydia or you. You're too well-liked. And who in the village would have wanted to kill Jason Lilywhite? He'd only been in Athelston two days. Apart from Jack Middlemarch, there wasn't a soul knew him.

Edwin (*snapping*) It didn't take him long to antagonize you.

Maurice (*heavily*) My grievance with him came after I found out the kind of man he was. (*Firmly*) You're not thinking straight and you're barking up the wrong tree.

Edwin (*coldly*) Maybe I am, but I don't think so. Somewhere in Bran's notebook is where I'm going to find out why someone's so anxious to stop the truth about Jason Lilywhite's death coming to light.

Maurice (*urgently*) Leave it alone.

Sheila enters, looking exasperated

Sheila (*to Edwin*) If you're not going to rest, you may as well have some lunch. It's all ready and it won't take a second to slice the bread.

Edwin (*testily*) I'm not hungry. I told you.

Sheila (*protesting*) It's lovely oxtail.

Edwin (*irritated*) Maybe later. I'll be in the spare room.

Edwin exits

There is an embarrassed silence as Sheila and Maurice look at each other

Sheila (*apologetically*) He's hardly eaten a thing all week. I know I can't cook like Ida, but nothing seems to tempt him.

Maurice (*forcing a smile*) Must be his training, Sheila. "Lead us not into temptation" and all that.

Sheila (*concerned*) I've tried him with fish, and last night with lamb, but he just pushes it round his plate and it ends up in the bin. (*She sighs deeply*) It's hardly worth doing the rabbits. But you might have skinned them for me. I never could get the hang of it.

Maurice (*lightly*) I'll gladly skin them for you, but it's not me you
should be thanking. I've not touched a coney in years.
Sheila (*surprised*) Must be Roy Steadman, then. Left them on the
draining board while my back was turned. (*Scornfully*) Trust him to
get rid of the evidence before anybody caught him. Makes me sick,
men like him roaming round the countryside, shooting anything that
moves. Poor little things.
Maurice More likely uses snares. He's not allowed a gun. Not with his
police record.
Sheila (*indignantly*) Well, he certainly shot these two. You can put your
finger in the holes.
Maurice (*puzzled*) Then perhaps they're not from him?
Sheila (*firmly*) Oh, they're his all right. There's been no one else here
all morning—except Lady Cranshawe, and I can't see her soiling her
dainty fingers with dead rabbits. If she'd left anything behind, it'd be
a pot of caviar or a pound of venison.
Maurice But where would he get a gun from? There's not a dealer in
miles would take the risk. It'd cost them their licence.
Sheila (*shrugging*) No use asking me. If I had my way, there'd be
nobody allowed to have them. Even the army. No guns, no war's the
way I look at it. Whoever invented them should be shot.

Edwin enters looking angry

Edwin (*to Sheila*) The things in the spare room. Mr Walsh's things.
Have you touched any of them?
Sheila (*flustered*) I've not been in there. Except to leave the sack.
Edwin (*accusingly*) You've not looked through the box on the bed?
Sheila (*shaking her head*) No.
Maurice (*to Edwin*) What is it? What's wrong?
Edwin It's Bran's notebook. It's gone.

They all look at each other as the Lights fade rapidly

SCENE 3

*The following evening. The room is unchanged, but the french
windows are closed, the curtains are drawn and the light is on. Edwin
is reclining on the settee, eyes closed, listening to the first movement of*
Tchaikovsky's Sixth Symphony

The door chime sounds. Reluctantly, he rises, moves to the door and exits

A few moments later he re-appears, followed by a pale looking Helen, who wears a dark summer coat over her dress. He crosses to the CD cabinet and turns the music off

Helen (*falteringly*) I'm sorry. I didn't mean to disturb you.
Edwin (*turning to her*) Just trying to relax. (*He indicates the settee*)
Helen (*moving round to it*) What was it? That you were listening to?
Edwin Tchaikovsky. Sixth Symphony.
Helen It's beautiful.
Edwin A bit maudlin, according to some. But it suited my mood. (*Indicating the settee*) Please.

Helen sits

Helen I expect you're wondering why I'm here?
Edwin (*shrugging*) There's been a constant stream of visitors since the news of my resignation got out. Can I offer you a drink? Tea? Coffee?
Helen No, thank you. I won't stay long. It's just that—well—I saw Maurice Walker this afternoon and he told me what you were thinking. That Jason's death was somehow related to Lydia's and Mr Walsh's. I came to tell you that you're wrong. It had nothing to do with them.
Edwin And you know that for a fact, do you?
Helen (*quietly*) Yes. I was married to David Lilywhite for nine years. He was kind, considerate, and the sweetest man I'd ever met. He wouldn't have harmed a fly. His only fault—if you could call it that—was that he idolized his brother. Despite everything that had happened, he wouldn't hear a word said against him.

Edwin sits in the armchair, R

As I told you some time ago, I didn't really like Jason. He made me uneasy. There was something—predatory about him and you'd hardly have known they were brothers if there hadn't been such a strong resemblance. (*She lapses into silence*)
Edwin (*after a moment*) And?
Helen (*rising*) He'd not been feeling well... David, I mean. We had serious financial problems in Lincoln and there was no way we could stay there. (*She moves* DL) The plan was that we'd sell up, pay off our debts, then find a small tea-room somewhere, and concentrate on catering. I wasn't a brilliant actress, but I was rather good in the cakes and pies department and David could act as front-of-house manager. He'd always kept in touch with Reverend Middlemarch, and when

he heard the tea-room here was up for sale, he jumped at the chance and came down to look it over. By the time he got home again, he had plans a mile high. (*Turning to face Edwin*) Then the blow fell. We found he had cancer. It was only a matter of months.

Edwin But obviously they were wrong.

Helen (*moving behind the settee*) Jason was about to be released so David went to see him, of course. To break the news in person. And that's when he got the idea. Jason had life insurance. Nearly half a million pounds of it, and when he died it would all be ours.

Edwin (*appalled*) You're not telling me David killed Jason?

Helen (*angrily*) Of course not. I told you. David loved him. He couldn't have harmed him if he'd wanted to.

Edwin So who did shoot him?

Helen (*quietly*) No one. (*Hesitating*) It was David who died, that night.

Edwin stares at her

(*Moving* L, *again*) He planned it down to the last detail. It had to be done in Athelston because too many people knew him in Lincoln and it was too late to do it anywhere else. We'd already signed the papers for the tea-room and he was finding it harder and harder to fight the pain. The second night we arrived, the locals hadn't had a chance to work out which of them was which, so that's when he decided it was time to act. I don't know where the gun came from. Jason had picked it up on his travels somewhere, and managed to keep it hidden when he went to jail. We watched the street from the bedroom and David waited on the landing. He was in so much pain he could hardly stand but we had to have a witness. The minute Henry Wilson came round the corner, Jason pointed the gun and pulled the trigger. (*Softly*) And David died.

Edwin (*after a moment*) So who ran out of the house?

Helen (*facing him*) Jason, of course. He turned away from Mr Wilson so he couldn't be recognized, ran into King's Lane, through the garden at twenty seven, over the fence and back into the house. By the time the police arrived, he'd changed into David's pyjamas and was cradling the body.

Edwin And what had he done with the gun? It was never found, I believe.

Helen (*hesitating*) I've no idea. I did ask him once but he told me it was none of my business. All I had to do was to keep up the pretence it was Jason who'd died, and he'd deal with the rest. I suppose he hid it again. He certainly didn't come back with it.

Edwin (*wonderingly*) So the whole thing was a façade?

Helen (*shaking her head*) The grief was genuine. He really was horrified by what he'd done. He couldn't stop shaking. They had to sedate him in order to separate them.

Edwin And what about you?

Helen (*matter-of-factly*) I was glad it was over. I'd done my best to talk him out of it, but he was slipping away by the hour. It broke my heart to hear him moaning with pain—and the drugs he had were almost useless. I couldn't let him suffer any longer. It wasn't just him his cancer was killing, it was me, too. But I'd made him a promise and I didn't intend to let him down. Much as I disliked Jason, I loved David more. The Cranshawe woman was right. He was killed by his brother, but she didn't realise he was the wrong victim. (*Looking down*)

Edwin (*after a pause*) And the scene in the quarry? Was she right about that, too? Or was it said out of malice?

Helen (*shaking her head*) He changed his mind. Jason, that is. Decided he couldn't do it. He may have been a crook, but he wasn't a killer. It was tearing him apart just thinking about it. He'd gone to the quarry to clear his head and David followed to plead with him. He'd been doubled up with pain that morning and wanted to get it over with.

Edwin And the (*hesitating*) other accusation?

Helen (*smiling wanly*) Jason had a tattoo—a rather explicit one—in the middle of his back. It was the one thing that could have given the game away. When he realised this, David had it copied. He'd been waiting for it to heal in order to put his plan in action, and took his shirt off to show Jason it was ready. If she'd waited a few more minutes, she'd have seen him dressing again, but she didn't, and drew the totally wrong conclusion.

Edwin And what about Jack Middlemarch? You must have known you'd never fool him. The minute he saw Jason, he'd know it was David who'd died.

Helen (*tiredly*) That was pure luck. He was away when we arrived in Athelston, so David wrote me a letter to take to him—begging him to cover up what we'd done. Jason was terrified, and said there wasn't a chance. He'd blow the plan sky high and we'd both go to jail. He couldn't go through that again. There had to be some other way of keeping him quiet. But David insisted and I agreed with him. When Jason came home from the hospital after the shooting, he was still in a state of shock and locked himself in his room for most of the day. The vicar was back by then, so I waited till evening and came over to see him.

Edwin (*heavily*) Only to find him dead.

Helen (*hesitating*) But—there was something else. Something I've never told anyone. (*Moving* R, *behind the settee again*) As I walked

towards the church, Jason came through the lychgate as though
someone was chasing him. I couldn't believe it. I'd no idea he'd even
left the house. I didn't want another argument, so I hid in Hanson's
doorway till he turned the corner, then made my way to the vestry as
quickly as I could. The reverend wasn't there, of course, but Henry
Wilson was and thought I might find him in the belfry. They'd been
practising there a little earlier. So we went round together and found
him. (*Quietly*) That's when I went to pieces. All I could hear was Jason
saying there had to be another way of silencing him, and all I could see
was him running away from the church just before I found the body.

Edwin (*stunned*) You mean—he'd killed Jack? It wasn't an accident?

Helen (*helplessly*) I don't know. It was just what I thought. He'd killed
David, so why not Reverend Middlemarch? The next thing I knew,
they were pumping me full of Valium again. Only this time it took me
a lot longer to be able to face the world.

Edwin Did you ask him about it, later? Tell him what you saw?

Helen (*shaking her head*) By the time I snapped out of it, I realized
there'd be nothing to gain. Everyone thought it was an accident, and
if I went to the police, everything we'd done was bound to come out.
Like it or not, I'd made my bed and now I had to sleep in it. The
insurance money came through, we paid off our debts, and as far
as anyone else was concerned, David and Helen Lilywhite put the
tragedy behind them and settled down to normal village life.

Edwin (*puzzled*) Then, why did you agree to let Bran write his book?
If he had gone ahead with it and discovered the truth, you'd certainly
have been arrested.

Helen (*wanly*) How could he have worked it out? It was the perfect
crime.

Edwin (*curious*) So why are you admitting it to me?

Helen (*tiredly*) As I said. You had to know that your wife's death—and
Mr Walsh's—had nothing to do with us.

Edwin But you realise I've got to tell the police what you've told me?

Helen (*shrugging*) It really doesn't matter. Jason's dead—and I won't
be far behind him.

Edwin looks at her blankly

(*With forced brightness*) Ovarian cancer. I got the results this morning.
By the time I get to trial, it won't be worth the bother.

Edwin (*at a loss*) I'm...sorry.

Helen (*smiling bleakly*) Look on it as God's punishment. (*Quoting*)
"Vengeance is mine, sayeth the Lord". Well he's certainly getting it
now.

Edwin (*rising*) Are you sure that nothing can be done?

Helen (*lightly*) You can put me next to David—the real David—when the time comes. (*Frowning*) Or would there be some objection? One's never too sure, the way things change from day to day. (*Grimacing*) I'd really hate to share my grave with the wrong man.

Edwin (*uncertainly*) I'll—have to take advice on that.

Helen (*briskly*) Right. I'd better be going. I'll be staying with my sister in Norwich for the next few weeks. After that—who knows? If you do call the police, I won't be too hard to find. (*She turns to exit*)

Edwin (*hastily*) Just one more thing.

She turns back to him

Your husb... I mean—Jason's death. (*He hesitates*) It really was an accident?

Helen (*frowning*) Of course it was. The edge of the quarry gave way and he fell. Why do you ask?

Edwin I just don't understand what was he doing there at that time of night. Without a torch.

Helen Yes. It puzzled us too. But I don't suppose we'll ever know.

The telephone begins to ring and he crosses to answer it

As he picks up the receiver, Helen quietly exits

Edwin (*tiredly*) Vicarage. ... No. No. It's all right. What can I do for you? ... I shouldn't think so. I'll be going to bed, shortly. You can drop them round to the Verger in the morning and he'll deal with them. (*He sighs*) Yes. Yes. Whenever's convenient. There's no hurry. Thank you, Mr Catchpole.

He replaces the receiver, closes his eyes for a moment, then crosses back to the CD player and turns it on

For a few seconds he stands there, gazing at the machine and listening to the music, then moves back to the door, opens it and exits

A few moments later, Roy sidles into the room, dressed in dark clothing and carrying a case

Roy (*entering*) Anybody home? (*He glances round the room then moves casually* R *in the direction of the CD player and picks up the CD case to study it*)

Edwin enters behind him, holding a glass of milk. He sees Roy

Edwin (*puzzled*) Roy?

Roy (*turning to him*) Oh, there you are, Vicar. Everything all right?

Edwin Why shouldn't it be? How did you get in? I didn't hear the chime.

Roy (*easily*) Noticed the front door was ajar as I passed. Thought there might be something wrong so I popped inside for a look.

Edwin (*shaking his head*) No. Everything's fine. The catch couldn't have caught when she left.

Roy Ah. (*Nods knowingly*) Been up to see you, has she? I noticed she was back. (*He puts the case down*)

Edwin (*frowning*) I'm sorry?

Roy Ida Cornish. The lights were on in her cottage.

Edwin (*shaking his head again*) Oh. No. It wasn't Ida. I've hardly seen her since I came out of hospital.

Roy (*smiling*) Must have been Helen Lilywhite, then? I thought I saw her crossing the street.

Edwin (*moving down to the settee*) It's really none of your business, Roy. Now if you wouldn't mind...? (*He sips at his milk as he sits*)

Roy turns off the music

(*Surprised*) What are you doing? (*He puts his glass on the coffee table*)

Roy (*easily*) It's a bit distracting. Trying to have a conversation when music's playing. Some'd say it was plain bad manners.

Edwin (*put out*) As far as I remember, we've nothing to converse about. And I happened to be listening to that, so if there's nothing else——

Roy (*cutting in*) How much did she tell you, Vicar? (*Warningly*) And don't try playing the innocent, because it wouldn't wash. She sent me a text, you see? Said she was on her way here because you had to know the truth.

Edwin (*hedging*) Truth? About what?

Roy (*flatly*) The night David Lilywhite died. (*Moving closer*) So let's stop beating round the bush and tell me what she said.

Edwin (*rising*) My conversation with Mrs Lilywhite is an entirely private matter, and I've no intention of telling you——

Roy grabs Edwin by the throat, choking him

Roy (*menacingly*) I asked you a question, Vicar. What did she tell you?

Edwin (*choking and trying to free himself*) He'd—fallen from the top of the quarry.

Roy (*disgustedly*) I mean the real David Lilywhite. Not his jailbird brother.

Edwin (*surprised*) You—know?

Roy (*coldly*) I've known since the night they killed him. (*He releases Edwin and moves* R *again*)

Edwin collapses on to the settee, clutching his throat

(*Chattily*) It's a funny thing, coincidence. Of all the jails in all the country, we had to do time in the same one. Only a few months, admittedly, but I recognized him the minute I saw him. Jason bloody Lilywhite. Tearing down the street with a shotgun in his hands. I couldn't believe my eyes.

Edwin (*shakily*) So Sheila was right. You did see something. (*He takes a sip of milk to soothe his throat*)

Roy A few more yards and he'd have knocked me over.

Edwin (*warily*) So—why didn't you tell the police?

Roy (*moving round the back of the settee*) I couldn't grass my old pal Jason up, could I? Not when I found out what game they were playing.

Edwin And—how did you do that? (*He massages his neck gently*)

Roy (*moving down* L) By dropping round to offer my condolences. He was quite accommodating when he realized I could blow the whole thing sky high, and told me the full story. It didn't take long for them to offer me a partnership, so to speak, and I got my share of the insurance money, while their naughty little secret stayed safe and sound.

Edwin But not from Jack Middlemarch.

Roy (*shaking his head sadly*) Pity about Jack. He wasn't a bad old stick, but he'd never have kept his mouth shut. Too outspoken for his own good. It didn't leave them any choice. He had to die.

Edwin (*sickened*) So Jason did push him down the belfry steps.

Roy frowns

Helen saw him running away. Just before she found the body.

Roy (*amused*) Jason didn't kill Middlemarch. (*Moving back behind the settee again, heading* R) He hadn't the guts to kill anybody.

Edwin He killed his brother.

Roy (*laughing*) She told you that? (*Incredulously*) And you believed her? (*Shaking his head*) What an actress. (*Harshly*) She shot the poor bugger herself. Gave him both barrels without a second thought.

Edwin (*stunned*) But...

Roy (*amused*) It was her idea that the brothers swapped identities. Not his. And he was so sick and under her thumb, he actually went along with it. She kept telling him he'd be (*mockingly*) "doing it for her", but all she really wanted was to get her hands on Jason's cash as quickly as possible. (*Sneering*) As for him—the poor bastard was so broken by five years in the pokey, he'd have done anything to stay on the outside. (*Flatly*) Helen pushed Middlemarch down the steps. Before she went looking for Henry Wilson. She needed a witness so they could find the body together.

Edwin (*shocked*) How do you know this?

Roy (*scowling*) I didn't know it—at the time. (*He sits on the arm of the chair*) It was only later—when she started coming on to me—that Jason let it slip.

Edwin (*startled*) You mean—you and Helen? (*He puts the milk down*)

Roy Why not? I knew Jason wasn't her husband. And she's not a bad looker. The only trouble was, we couldn't risk being seen together. Not in this village. (*Standing*) We used to meet in the Prentice quarry. (*He moves behind the settee again*) I wanted her to marry me, but she kept backing off. Said it'd look suspicious if she left "David" and took up with a reprobate like me. The only way it could work out for us was if he died as well. After that...we could leave the village and it'd only be a matter of time.

Edwin (*dully*) So she pushed him into the quarry?

Roy (*shaking his head*) That was me.

Edwin looks startled

I lured him up there and tipped him over the edge while she pretended to be looking for him. (*Moving down* L) Quite a girl, the lovely Helen.

Edwin (*uneasily*) Why are you telling me this?

Roy (*sitting on the chair arm*) For the past few weeks, she's not been—well—let's say as passionate as usual. Breaking dates—and trotting out excuses a ten year old wouldn't fall for. (*Smiling*) So, being of a suspicious nature, I decided to keep an eye on her and see what she was up to. And guess what? She's playing around with our genial local landlord, (*snarling*) Mr Maurice "Stuck-Up" Walker.

Edwin (*puzzled*) I still don't see...

Roy (*standing*) So when she sent me that text tonight, and knowing how devious her mind is, the old alarm bell started ringing. (*Moving behind the settee*) What if her version of "the truth", happened to be the one where I'd killed everybody and she was as innocent as a new-born babe?

Edwin (*frowning*) She never even mentioned you.

Roy (*reasonably*) But I didn't know that, did I? (*Moving down* R) As far as I knew, as soon as she'd finished her story, you'd be on the phone to the police and I'd be looking at life imprisonment. (*Bitterly*) I'd always wanted a gun of my own and I'd taken the one she used on David for poaching. Got it stashed up the bedroom chimney with my prints all over it. If they found that, I was done for.

Edwin (*uneasily*) So...?

Roy Now I'm in a quandry. (*Looking at Edwin, thoughtfully*) What do I do about you? Wouldn't make sense to just walk away and hope you'd keep your mouth shut. Not now you know the full story.

Edwin (*quietly*) Not quite the full story.

Roy (*frowning*) Is there something I've missed?

Edwin (*rising*) Who poisoned Lydia's casserole? Have you thought about that? (*He moves* L, *round the settee and upstage*)

Roy (*hastily*) No, you don't. (*He moves round the settee to stop him using the telephone, and pulls out the wire*)

Edwin (*surprised*) I was getting a drink. You've bruised my throat and I need something stronger than milk. (*Stooping to get a bottle of brandy from the cabinet*) You haven't answered my question.

Roy (*relaxing*) I don't understand it. She did it herself, didn't she?

Edwin (*getting a glass*) No. She was poisoned deliberately. We all were. (*He pours a drink*)

Roy What makes you so sure?

Edwin (*scornfully*) She wasn't a fool. No way would she mistake yew spines for rosemary. Somebody else doctored that casserole. With cold-blooded murder in mind.

Roy It was nothing to do with us.

Edwin You weren't trying to stop Bran researching his book?

Roy (*puzzled*) Why should we? He couldn't have proved anything.

Edwin So you've no idea why it happened? (*He looks at the glass in his hand and gives an enquiring look at Roy*)

Roy nods and Edwin gives Roy his glass and fetches another

Roy We'd nothing against you. We thought it was an accident.

Edwin (*pouring*) And that's what people were meant to think. An unfortunate accident. (*Putting the bottle down*) The whole village knew she couldn't cook for toffee, so the timing was perfect. All three of us dead, and Lydia would take the blame. (*He gazes into his glass*)

Roy (*after a moment*) No. It doesn't make sense. Who'd want to poison you three? Where's the motive? (*He gulps his drink*)

Edwin We all have motives, Roy. (*Moving down* L) Some more than others. Yours are based on greed and lust, and mine—well—mine are more complicated. (*Sitting in the armchair*) You're thinking of killing me, aren't you?

Roy (*admiringly*) Don't miss a trick, do you? It's nothing personal, but I haven't a choice. I'm too old to go back inside. (*He finishes the drink, and puts the glass down before moving towards Edwin*) But you've always treated me decently—you and the Missus—so I'll make it as painless as possible. It's nice and dark now so why don't we take a stroll to the bell-tower and look at the stars from the top?

Edwin (*mildly*) There's really no need. To kill me, I mean. I won't tell anyone.

Roy (*sadly*) But can I be certain? I don't think so.

Edwin Even if I tell you I poisoned Ida's casserole?

Roy (*halting*) Eh?

Edwin It was me who killed Lydia and Bran. (*He puts his glass down and rises*) She was pregnant when I married her, and wouldn't tell me the father's name. But I didn't care. I loved her more than anything else in the world and the only thing I wanted was to be with her. (*Moving behind the settee*) I was devastated when she lost the baby, but at least I still had her. We were still together. Then early this year I found a letter from Bran and realised the baby was his. Her own cousin. Not only that, but the affair was still going on, and had been for years. I couldn't believe it. The only reason she'd married me was because Brandon wouldn't commit to her. It tore me apart. My wife and my oldest friend were laughing behind my back and I wanted revenge. They didn't suspect, of course. Thought they were far too clever to be found out by a stupid village priest. That's when I made my mind up. I invited him here to check out the Lilywhite murder, but I couldn't have cared less about a book he might write. He'd never have time to finish it.

There is a pause

Roy (*curious*) So what happened next?

Edwin (*reviving*) It had to look like an accident, of course. And I knew how poisonous yew trees are. We'd a case in my last parish. Children eating the berries in the graveyard. Two of them recovered, but the other died. The rest of the tree's far more deadly, as I'm sure you know. I made up a small amount of poison and waited for an opportunity to do what I had to. Ida's casserole was the perfect medium and a few yew spines only added to the legend of Lydia's appalling culinary skills.

Roy (*frowning*) But you ate it yourself. You almost died.

Edwin (*smiling*) I fully intended to. Without her, there was no reason to go on living. Even now, I'm unsure if my survival has any real purpose.

Roy And what if it hadn't worked out? If they hadn't died, and she'd been able to tell the police it was nothing to do with her?

Edwin (*moving* L) Highly unlikely. They both had healthy appetites and I gave Bran an extra dose in his after dinner drink, just to make sure. But I had foreseen the possibility. He was here to write a book—a book that several people in the village weren't too happy about. If one of them killed David Lilywhite, and thought the truth might come out if Bran dug hard enough, it could well appear the intended victim was him. Lyd and I would be incidental. The trick, of course, was to make the link obvious, so I took the cymbals from the Memorial Hall and tied them to Henry's doorknocker.

Roy (*puzzled*) And how would that help?

Edwin (*amused*) Don't tell me you haven't worked it out? Lyd and I have joked about it since the day we got here. The Lilywhite boys... the Walker family and their pub. Sheila Pashley's been singing it under her breath for months. If anything had gone wrong, the police would have been looking for a killer with a peculiar sense of humour and a fondness for folk songs. (*Smiling wanly*) So there you have it. A full and complete confession. (*He sits in the armchair* L)

Roy And what am I expected to do with it?

Edwin (*mildly*) It's up to you. If you go to the police, I'll be arrested and jailed. And if I tell the police your part in the Lilywhite saga, you'll be joining me. Something of a stalemate, wouldn't you say?

Roy (*after a moment's thought*) Looks like we needn't take that stroll, then. Too many clouds for stargazing, anyway. (*Easily*) Not bad for rabbits, though. Might take a trip to the quarry and see what's happening. (*He moves towards the door, opens it, then pauses*) Thanks for the drink. And watch that door-catch, Vicar. You never know who could walk in all unexpected. See you tomorrow.

Roy exits, closing the door

Edwin (*softly*) I don't think so, Roy. (*He picks up his glass, looks at it and smiles*) I somehow don't think so. (*He rises and crosses to the CD cabinet, puts the glass down, opens the curtains and windows and stands gazing into the darkened garden*)

Behind him, the door opens and Ida moves into the room with an expressionless face. She carries a thick notebook

Edwin turns to see her

(*Surprised*) Ida.

Ida (*flatly*) I heard you were looking for this. (*She holds out the notebook*)

Edwin (*puzzled*) What is it?

Ida Mr Walsh's notebook.

Edwin stares at it

I thought I'd make an early start tomorrow, so when I got back, I called on Sheila to collect the vicarage keys. (*Accusingly*) I found her in a real state. You'd as much as accused her of stealing without actually saying it, and she was crying her eyes out with shock. (*Stoutly*) Well, I wasn't having that, vicar or no vicar. She might be many things, Sheila Pashley, but she's definitely not a thief. The first thing I did was to tell her to get her coat on and come round here for an apology.

Edwin (*soothingly*) I'm terribly sorry, Ida. I'd no right to take it out on her. I wasn't thinking straight and she was right in the line of fire. Of course I'll apologize. I wouldn't upset her for the world. Where is she?

Ida Gone to call the police.

Edwin (*flustered*) But that's ridiculous. She can't call in the police because I've hurt her feelings. And you still haven't told me where you found the notebook.

Ida When we let ourselves in, you had a visitor.

Edwin looks shocked

We could hear you talking, and didn't want to make a scene with outsiders present, so we went upstairs to see if we could find it. And we did. (*Showing Edwin the book*) The box on the bed had tipped over, and we found it under the cabinet. It hadn't gone missing at all.

Edwin (*shrugging*) As I told you, I wasn't feeling too good. I must have overlooked it. It's not that important, anyway.

Ida So why make such a fuss about it?

Edwin (*sighing*) All right. (*Explaining*) Gwendolyn Cranshawe was trying to get her hands on it. She wanted someone else to write Bran's book using his notes and she's the last person in the world I wanted to have it. I thought if I made out it had been stolen, she'd drop the whole idea.

Ida But there never was going to be a book, was there, Vicar? We heard you telling Roy.

Edwin stares at her

The door was ajar when we came downstairs. We heard every word.

That's why Sheila's calling the police. Not because you upset her. (*Sharply*) By this time tomorrow, you'll both be under arrest.

Edwin (*smiling sadly*) I don't think so, Ida. By this time tomorrow, they'll be far too late. (*Moving* DR) I really did love Lydia, and there's nothing left for me now that she's gone. I've been wanting to join her ever since I left the hospital. That's why I added the last of the poison to the brandy. Taking Roy with me seemed a very good idea and the murderous Helen's got her own problems. If we are going to be judged, it'll be in a far higher court than anything here on earth. (*He picks up his glass and drains the liquid*) Thank you for being so kind.

Ida stares at him, then realising what he has done, picks up the phone and finds it is dead. Hastily she replaces it

Ida hurries out of the room

(*Singing softly*) "Two, two the Lilywhite boys .. Clothèd all in green, O-O... One is one and all alone... And evermore shall be so..."

The lights slowly fade to Black-out

FURNITURE AND PROPERTY LIST

ACT I
SCENE 1

On stage: Record/CD cabinet supporting a dated-looking sound system
Large cabinet containing various drinks bottles including brandy,
glasses, knick-knacks, two liqueur glasses
Small glass-fronted cabinet containing ancient books. *On it:* small
table lamp, a pile of books
Upright piano with closed lid. *On it:* books, sheet music. *Beneath
it:* box piano stool
Large bookcase crammed with ancient tomes. *On it:* hideous vase
filled with fresh flowers
Settee
Narrow table. *On it:* telephone, various ornaments
Long coffee table. *On it* R: books, open box of chocolates
Two armchairs
Threadbare carpet
Framed pictures on the walls
Light switch L of the door
Hall
Garden
Staircase
French windows and drapes
Fireplace

Off stage: Duster (**Ida**)
Tray of tea things containing cups and saucers (**Ida**)
Tea pot (**Ida**)
Tray holding two glasses of lager and one of lemonade (**Lydia**)

Personal: **Roy**: mobile phone
Lydia: handbag

SCENE 2

Re-set: Fresh flowers in the vase
Books and magazines
French windows open, door closed
Strike: Glasses and tea things, box of chocolates

Set: Battered-looking book and A4 notepad, pen

Off stage: Tray containing a mug of coffee and a doughnut on a plate (**Ida**)
Large shopping bag. *In it:* a hard-backed book and a large manilla envelope (**Sheila**)
Large shopping bag. *In it:* Sliced ham, potato salad, coleslaw, tin of pears (**Lydia**)
Mug of coffee, Mars Bar (**Lydia**)
Overnight bag, set of car keys (**Brandon**)

ACT II
SCENE 1

Re-set: French windows closed, door ajar

Strike: Crockery
Overnight bag

Off stage: Covered dish, a set of housekeys (**Ida**)

SCENE 2

Re-set: Fresh flowers in the vase
French windows open

Strike: Drinks and bottle

Off stage: Tray holding tea things including a tea pot, mugs and a plate of sliced fruit cake (**Sheila**)
Small jar of honey (**Gwendolyn**)

Personal: **Gwendolyn**: watch

SCENE 3

Re-set: French windows closed and curtains are drawn

Off stage: Glass of milk (**Edwin**)
Thick notebook (**Ida**)

LIGHTING PLOT

Property fittings required: light switch operating the central light
One interior set

ACT I, SCENE 1

To open: Bright general interior lighting

Cue 1   **Edwin** and **Lydia** stare at **Brandon**   (Page 17)
          Black-out

ACT I, SCENE 2

To open: Bright general interior lighting

Cue 2   **Edwin, Lydia** and **Brandon** all laugh happily   (Page 37)
          Fade to Black-out

ACT II, SCENE 1

To open: Fading daylight and lights are off. Light from the hall seeps in

Cue 3   **Lydia** enters, turning on the lights   (Page 38)
          Lights on

Cue 4   **Ida** screams   (Page 47)
          Lights fade rapidly to Black-out

ACT II, SCENE 2

To open: Bright general interior lighting

Cue 5   **Edwin, Sheila** and **Maurice** look at each other   (Page 60)
          Rapid fade as the CURTAIN *closes*

ACT II, SCENE 3

To open: Evening interior lighting

Cue 6   **Edwin**: "...And evermore shall be so..."   (Page 73)
          Lights fade to Black-out

EFFECTS PLOT

ACT I

Cue 14	**Maurice**: "Are you fixed for tonight, then?" *Hammering stops*	(Page 24)
Cue 15	**Lydia**: "...I'm eating it myself." *Door chimes sound*	(Page 31)

ACT II

Cue 16	**Brandon** sips at his drink *Door chimes sound*	(Page 39)
Cue 17	**Edwin**: "...she thought you might find it interesting." *Door chimes sound*	(Page 40)
Cue 18	**Edwin**: "...She said she'd bring it round tonight." *Door chimes sound*	(Page 40)
Cue 19	**Brandon**: "...he'll be right as rain." *Door chimes sound urgently*	(Page 43)
Cue 20	**Brandon** hurries to the phone and begins to dial *Door chimes sound*	(Page 45)
Cue 21	To open Scene 2 *Sound of a lawnmower*	(Page 47)
Cue 22	**Sheila** begins pouring tea into mugs *Sound of the mower dies*	(Page 47)
Cue 23	**Sheila** takes a hasty gulp of tea *Sound of door chimes*	(Page 50)
Cue 24	**Sheila**: "...not a mile away, this minute——" *Door chimes sound*	(Page 55)
Cue 25	To open Scene 3 *The first movement of Tchaikovsky's Sixth Symphony*	(Page 60)
Cue 26	After a few moments *Door chime sounds*	(Page 60)
Cue 27	**Edwin** turns the music off *Music off*	(Page 61)

Cue 28	**Helen**: "...But I don't suppose we'll ever know." *Telephone rings*	(Page 65)
Cue 29	**Edwin** turns the music on *Music on*	(Page 65)
Cue 30	**Roy** turn off the music *Music off*	(Page 66)